THE HOW TO KEEP HIM

(*After You've Caught Him*)

COOKBOOK

OTHER BOOKS BY JINX KRAGEN AND JUDY PERRY

Saucepans and the Single Girl

THE
HOW
TO
KEEP
HIM
(After You've Caught Him)
COOKBOOK

by Jinx Kragen and Judy Perry

Illustrated by John Alcorn

DOUBLEDAY & COMPANY, INC.
Garden City, New York
1968

When we think of skinned knees,
measles, D's in Biology, broken
hearts, tuition, clothes allow-
ances and going steady, all we
can say is

To our Parents
With love and thanks

ACKNOWLEDGMENT

Our thanks once again to our husbands Ken and Jack for manfully bearing up under a deluge of recipe-testing that would have sent lesser men packing.

CONTENTS

INTRODUCTION

or:

Here We Are Again

A lot has happened since we last pulled ourselves together to write a book. That book, which we called *Saucepans and the Single Girl,* was written about our guileless days of non-wedded bliss. In the interim we have acquired two husbands, two dogs and one baby (to which only one of us can claim credit, lest there be any confusion concerning our living arrangement). We've moved a total of 6,000 miles and have run through enough houses to guarantee the college educations of several real estate brokers' offspring.

Suspecting as we do that you have probably followed a similar path in the last few years or are about to embark on the great adventure, we have decided that the time has come again to put down a few random ideas for our comrades-in-arms. Not that we are experts, mind you, but we are realistic.

We know that there are days when that tide of laundry, dishes and coffee grounds not only seems like a lot of backwash but leaves you feeling like the little Dutch boy with his finger in the dike. You *know* that if you don't stay on red alert it'll all come rolling in again tomorrow.

But if, like us, you refuse to resign yourself to the suburban slag heap, raise the flag and read on.

Looking down from our exalted plateau of four years of experience, we have come to the startling conclusion that the most important thing about marriage is your husband. Granted, that seems an obvious conclusion, but one that can be too easily overlooked in the quagmire of trivia that overwhelms you. Surely you didn't walk down the aisle just to have the opportunity to win a Bake-Off or scrub a floor. You got married because you met some dashing young man with icy blue eyes, or shaggy hair or a dueling scar or whatever it is that appeals to you.

It's true that men are much maligned, and at times rightfully so, as thoughtless, feckless creatures. But perhaps the reason that we have considered them thoughtless is that we've been putting the emphasis on the wrong things. Men just don't notice whether or not you starch the tea towels. He'll never know or care if you make a ditty bag out of old napkins in which you can store unused jar rings. Honestly. What he does care about is what goes into his stomach, that you still look like the girl for whom he gave up his precious bachelor days and that you don't greet him at the gate with an inventory of domestic difficulties.

It's important, then, to keep an eye on the target and lift your gaze past the washing machine. If you find that some of the shine has faded from your hearthside, a little polish will restore the patina. And that's what this book is all about. Polishing, pampering and taking care of your man.

TECHNICAL DIFFICULTIES

Servings: We can't take a pledge that our estimates of numbers of servings will be correct for your family. After all, we have no way of knowing whether your man eats like a Viking or a sparrow. All we can say is that the servings we've listed are what we've found to work for us.

Symbols: That mysterious symbol (*) you'll find strewn throughout the book simply means that at this point you can refrigerate whatever it is and retrieve it for warming whenever the spirit moves you.

Blenders: We have heartlessly called for the use of an electric blender in a few recipes here and there. If you don't own one, there are several avenues of escape open to you. You can either gazelle on down to the appliance store and buy one or throw this book away right now. Or maybe just write us a nasty letter.

Saucepans and Spouses

1.

SAUCEPANS
AND
SPOUSES

In *Saucepans and the Single Girl,* we blithely lumped great batches of men in a dozen or so not entirely flattering niches. Not long after, our husbands became a trifle cool and worse, there were rumors of insurrection flying about the men's locker room at the golf club. The butcher started saving his worst sinewy steaks just for us and the mailman even took to boycotting our Occupant mail. A girl has to watch herself these days.

But to show that we will not be cowed by such tactics, we're courageously revisiting our men again in this book. In this second look our men undergo post-marital analysis and we've tried to give you some ideas as to what to feed your man—no matter what type he is. We ask only one thing. This time keep your copy of the book under lock and key. We can't eat tough steaks forever.

The Man in a Brooks Brothers Suit

If you've wooed and won that Madison Avenue man and your sales campaign is over at last, you're probably feeling quite smug and assured now that you have the key to his washroom. Just because he was a hard sell doesn't mean that your job is over—recall that even the biggest firms continue to work on new packaging even if sales are soaring.

Your martinis should rival those of the Steuben Room and your table must be a layout that would make Foote, Cone and Belding Kelly green. This man definitely does not want to hear about Mrs. Farmer's Country Day School. He wants to talk about the corporate ladder or the new Oxydol spot or maybe just himself. If you'll merely listen and refill his glass once in a while, he'll spend less time in Dinty Moore's and more hours in Darien.

The following menu should send him galloping straight past the Ad Club lounge on his way to catch the 5:48.

MADISON AVENUE MADRILENE

VEAL SALTIMBOCCA

FRESH ASPARAGUS

CHAIRMAN'S CHEESECAKE

MOUTON ROTHSCHILD

MADISON AVENUE MADRILENE

1 12-ounce can jellied red   *¼ teaspoon curry powder*
  consommé madrilene   *1 tablespoon red caviar*
¼ cup sour cream

Chill madrilene 3–4 hours. Spoon into your most splendid glass bowls. Add a dollop of sour cream, sprinkle with curry powder and a little red caviar. *Serves 2.*

VEAL SALTIMBOCCA

1 pound veal, cut and   *As many pieces of prosciutto*
 pounded for scallopini *as you have veal scallops*
Salt and pepper   *1½ tablespoons butter*
½ teaspoon sage   *4 tablespoons Marsala wine*
          1½ more tablespoons butter

Have the jovial red-cheeked butcher cut and pound the veal for you. Salt and pepper lightly and sprinkle sparingly with sage. Place a piece of prosciutto trimmed to fit the scallop on each one and secure with a toothpick. Sauté in 1½ tablespoons butter over high heat very quickly—about 90 seconds on each side. Place the scallops on a warm serving dish with ham side up. Add Marsala and butter to pan drippings and bring just to the boiling point. Scrape drippings from the bottom of the pan as you stir constantly. Pour sauce over meat and carry with pardonable pride to the table. *Serves 2.*

FRESH ASPARAGUS

1 dozen stalks very fresh asparagus
Water

Rinse the asparagus in cold water quickly. Snap off thick woody ends (they'll snap just at the tender point of their own accord). Gather stalks together and bind in one or two places (not on those tender tips) with strips of aluminum foil. Stand the bundle or bundles upright in about 1–2 inches of water in a saucepan. Cover tightly and simmer over medium–low heat for 10 minutes or less. This cooks the thick bottom of the stalk and only steams the tender tips to prevent that soggy, falling-apart effect. Serve just with butter—don't smother the wonderful, delicate flavor with hollandaise or sauces of that ilk. *Serves 2.*

CHAIRMAN'S CHEESECAKE

CRUST:

1 ½ cups graham cracker
  crumbs (or zwieback, stale
  cookies, etc.)

¼ cup sugar
½ cup butter, melted

FILLING:

8 ounces sour cream
2 teaspoons vanilla
4 eggs
½ cup sugar

2 tablespoons instant flour
¼ teaspoon salt
2 8-ounce packages cream
  cheese, softened

1 ½ cups strawberry preserves

Mix crust ingredients, press into bottom of spring form pan (9 inch) and chill while you're mixing the filling. Put all filling ingredients except the cream cheese into the blender and blend until smooth. Cut the cream cheese into small pieces and add. Blend at high speed until smooth. Pour slowly over crust and bake 1 hour at 325 degrees. Chill thoroughly. Smear preserves over the top. Chill another 2–3 hours. *Serves 10.*

Man's Man

Men's men should really be confined to girlish phases and never to matrimony, for they often make unfortunate mates. If you did marry your plaid-shirted camel driver, we can only wish you well. We won't even mention that two-week pack trip that passed for a honeymoon. We already know who carried the pack.

When you were courting, all those grouses (grice?) and rainbow trout seemed such an impressive masculine offering. But now when old leather-patches continues to crowd out your Metrecal with his brace of mallards, you can get pretty tired of the whole dreary parade.

What's more, it's additionally depressing to find that your

gourmet cookbook proclaims in five-color layouts that the only way to prepare salmon is to truss it and truffle it and aspic it to death. And then serve it cold—with its eyes wide open!

The following menu should enable you to sail through any season with nary a qualm and even get the house aired out before Tuesday's bridge luncheon.

One more thing: say a prayer that those prurient salmon don't make it upstream this time, else you be gifted with their progeny next year.

AVOCADO WITH PROSCIUTTO

SALMON À LA RUSSE

or

GLAZED DUCK IN THE PINK

or

STEAK AU POIVRE

BRUSSELS SPROUTS   HERB TOASTS

ALL-AMERICAN APPLESAUCE CAKE

LEMON-CHEESE SAUCE

CHÂTEAUNEUF DU PAPE

AVOCADO WITH PROSCIUTTO

½ large avocado
4 pieces prosciutto ham

Peel the half avocado and cut lengthwise into 4 pieces. Wrap each piece in a slice of prosciutto and anchor with a toothpick. Chill. *Serves 2.*

SALMON À LA RUSSE

3 anchovy filets   *1 large salmon steak*
2 tablespoons sweet butter   *1 tablespoon olive oil*
⅛ teaspoon paprika   *1 tablespoon black caviar*
Salt and pepper to taste

Blend anchovies, butter and paprika together until smooth. Salt and pepper steak and brush lightly with oil. Broil just until a fork slips through easily. Smear the butter mixture over the salmon steak. Sprinkle with caviar. *Serves 2.*

GLAZED DUCK IN THE PINK

1 duck, quartered	*¼ teaspoon salt*
¼ teaspoon ginger	*⅛ teaspoon pepper*

SAUCE:

1 8-ounce jar currant jelly
⅔ cup orange juice
1 tablespoon orange brandy

Have the butcher take care of all the messy quartering and trimming for you or if your man actually shot that defenseless bird out of the sky, hand it to him to take care of. Season the thing with ginger, salt and pepper. Roast, fatty side up, for 2 hours at 325 degrees. Reduce heat to 300 degrees, combine sauce ingredients and baste frequently for another hour. *Serves 2.*

And just in case he had a rough day at the blind:

STEAK AU POIVRE

1 enormous sirloin steak,   1 tablespoon seasoned pepper
about 1½ inches thick   Salt
2 tablespoons coarse ground
pepper

Bring the steak to room temperature. Trim excess fat from around the edges and score fat at 2-inch intervals to prevent curling. With the heel of your palm, rub coarse ground pepper and seasoned pepper well into the surfaces of the steak. Let stand for at least an hour. Broil near a hot flame until it reaches desired doneness. Season with salt and serve. *Serves 2 gluttons.*

HERB TOASTS

6 slices thin-sliced sandwich
  bread (*the soft, flabby
  kind*)
½ stick butter, softened

1 tablespoon chopped chives
¼ teaspoon each basil, thyme,
  savory

Trim crusts from bread. Combine softened butter with herbs. Spread bread slices and roll up, anchoring with a toothpick. Bake 25 minutes at 325 degrees. *Serves 2.*

ALL-AMERICAN APPLESAUCE CAKE

1¾ cups flour
1¼ teaspoons baking powder
½ teaspoon baking soda
¾ teaspoon cinnamon
Dash nutmeg
½ teaspoon salt

½ cup butter
1 cup sugar
2 eggs
1 cup applesauce
⅔ cup raisins
¾ cup chopped nuts

Sift together flour, baking powder, baking soda, cinnamon, nutmeg and salt. Cream butter and sugar together until fluffy. Add eggs separately to butter and sugar mixture, beating after each one. Blend in dry mixture. Add remaining ingredients and bake in a 9×5-inch loaf pan (greased) at 350 degrees for 1 hour, 15 minutes. After loaf has cooled, slice in 1-inch slices and serve warm with Lemon-Cheese Sauce. *Serves 8.*

LEMON-CHEESE SAUCE

1 8-ounce package cream
  cheese, softened
1 cup powdered sugar
⅛ teaspoon salt

1 teaspoon grated lemon peel
2 tablespoons lemon juice
7 tablespoons orange juice

Combine all ingredients and beat until very smooth. Serve chilled over All-American Applesauce Cake or leftover gingerbread. *Makes 2 cups.*

The Man in a Garret

If you married that velvet-jacketed descendant of The Bard himself, your life is probably much like a ride on a yo-yo. Men in garrets are sporadically rich and poor, depending on whether the Literary Guild is buying this month or the Guggenheim has some empty wall space. Being romantics, garret men are never ones to hoard away their pennies for that oft-heralded drizzly day. Learn to savor your brief flirtations with affluence and try to prepare yourself for the leaner days ahead. Remember the compensations; just as you're beginning to walk on your lower lip, he'll tell you that you have a smile that's a dead ringer for the Mona Lisa and there you'll be—weak and wobbly in the knees.

Not only will his checkbook balance vacillate like an EKG, but so will his spirit and it's up to you to be his Gibraltar. He honestly does think he's going to write another *Gatsby* and you absolutely must not laugh when the first chapter sounds like a steal from *Dick and Jane*. He'll be jubilant when you inspire him on to bigger and better canvases or will swear like a trencherman when his typewriter ribbon breaks right in the middle of the denouement scene.

But if this is a good month and no rejection slips have peppered the mail, you're probably celebrating and feeling highly speculative. Here's a menu designed to spur him on to even greater heights:

GARRET GRAPEFRUIT

GAM OF LAMB   ZUCCHINI SOUFFLÉ

SCARLETT O'HARA

CABERNET SAUVIGNON

GARRET GRAPEFRUIT

1 grapefruit, halved and sectioned
Dry vermouth

Sprinkle cut sides of grapefruit with a whiff of vermouth and broil until just golden. *Serves 2.*

GAM OF LAMB

1 4-pound bone-in leg of   *Salt and pepper*
   lamb   *1 cup dry white wine*
2 cloves garlic, split

Rub fatty side of lamb with cloves of garlic and rub in salt and pepper with the heel of your palm. Put the lamb, fatty side up, in a roasting pan without a rack. Jam in your meat thermometer. Pour the wine in the bottom of the pan and roast at 350 degrees, basting occasionally, until the meat thermometer reads 180 degrees. *Serves 6.*

ZUCCHINI SOUFFLÉ

2 pounds zucchini, sliced and   *½ pound sharp Cheddar*
   cooked   *cheese, grated*
1 clove garlic, crushed   *Buttered bread crumbs*
18 soda crackers, crushed   *Parmesan cheese*
3 eggs, separated   *Paprika*

Mix drained, cooked squash, garlic, soda crackers, beaten egg yolks and cheese together, using a potato masher. Beat whites until stiff and fold into mixture. Pour into buttered casserole or soufflé dish. Top with sprinklings of buttered bread crumbs, Parmesan and paprika. Bake 45 minutes at 325 degrees. *Serves 6.*

SCARLETT O'HARA

You can bet Scarlett didn't keep her 14-inch waistline on a steady diet of this, but a little of this gooey Southern dessert *will* turn old Harold into another Rhett—at least while it lasts.

4 ounces sweet chocolate	Dash salt
¼ cup butter	2 eggs
1 tall can evaporated milk	1 teaspoon vanilla
(1⅔ cups)	1 can flaked coconut (1⅓
1½ cups sugar	cups)
3 tablespoons cornstarch	¾ cup chopped pecans

Melt chocolate and butter together over low heat, stirring constantly until well blended. Remove and gradually add milk. Mix dry ingredients together and beat in eggs and vanilla. Blend in chocolate mixture and pour into 8-inch-square pan. Combine coconut and nuts and sprinkle over batter. Bake at 375 degrees for 55 minutes or until top puffs up and cracks slightly. Cool 2–3 hours. *Serves 6.*

And then there are the lean months when you haven't got the price of a new set of coffee grounds:

CRISP RAW VEGETABLES
WEEKDAY WEAKNESS
COFFEE COROT

WEEKDAY WEAKNESS

3 tablespoons butter	1½ pounds elbow macaroni,
3 tablespoons flour	cooked and drained
2 cups milk, room tempera-	10 slices bacon, drained and
ture	crumbled
Salt and pepper to taste	½ cup cubed Cheddar cheese
2½ cups grated Cheddar	1 tomato, sliced
cheese	

Melt butter in skillet and stir in flour. Cook 1 minute. Add milk slowly, stirring constantly until thick. Season with salt and pepper. Add 2 cups of the grated cheese and stir until melted and well blended. Mix cheese sauce with cooked macaroni. In a greased 13×9×2-inch pan, place a layer of the macaroni-cheese mixture and sprinkle with crumbled bacon and a few of the cubes of cheese. Repeat process until you run out of something. Sprinkle top with remaining ½ cup of grated cheese. Arrange tomato slices, wedging them halfway down into macaroni and cheese. Bake at 350 degrees for 25 minutes or until you just can't wait any longer. *Serves 6–8.*

COFFEE COROT

Strong black coffee　　　　*Granulated sugar*
Dark rum　　　　　　　　*Brown sugar*
Vanilla ice cream

For each serving fill a large mug ¾ full of coffee. Stir in 1 ounce dark rum and top each with a scoop of ice cream. Sprinkle ice cream with a little of each of the sugars.

Lover with a Leica

One of the more unpleasant facts of life for the girl who marries a journalist is that the only estate she'll ever have is the Fourth. Even the excitement of being on the Big Story will be small comfort when you feel the wolf's hot breath under the weather stripping.

Of course, there is always the outside chance—however remote —that by now your green-visored copy boy has risen to the level of an urbane foreign correspondent, dashing from one world capital to another. If such is the case, the last thing you need is a homely bit of advice from us on how to make a casserole on two chicken bones and a slice of day-old bread. But for the most part, unless you're Huntley's helpmate or Brinkley's better half you're probably going to be field-mouse poor forevermore. Either take in washing or resign yourself to lots of pasta and an occasional bowl of good thick soup to take the chill off his typing fingers.

An editorial note: Your newspaperman is an intense soul and you just *think* he's not noticing that your hair is lank and your nails scruffy. He sees it all right; you're forgetting that even Clark Kent had X-ray vision. So if he's been mumbling about Brenda Starr in his sleep, it's time to put down the Sunday funnies and leap to the larder. Since you wooed him on Senate Bean Soup, here's a slight change of pace that's good enough to rate an invitation to see his darkroom. And don't forget to comb your hair.

LUSCIOUS LENTIL SOUP

BY-LINE BISCUITS   TOSSED SALAD

PINEAPPLE AVEDON

BEER

LUSCIOUS LENTIL SOUP

1 pound dried lentils
1 cup smoked sausage, torn in small pieces
1 clove garlic, minced
1 medium onion, chopped
¾ cup chopped celery with tops

3 quarts water
1 1-pound can solid pack tomatoes with juice
¼ cup chopped green pepper
Salt and pepper

Soak lentils 3–4 hours or overnight in cold water to cover. Drain. Put lentils in large soup kettle with all remaining ingredients except tomatoes and green pepper. Simmer heftily for 3–4 hours. Sieve if desired. Add tomatoes and green pepper and simmer another 30 minutes. Season to taste. Serve hot to two and just pray that your dog likes lentil soup too. But then this is pretty good—your mild-mannered reporter will probably eat it all and won't be able to skinny into that phone booth again.

BY-LINE BISCUITS

Follow the directions for drop biscuits on that beloved box of biscuit mix. Just before dropping by spoonfuls onto a cookie sheet or old developing pan, add a goodly handful of crumbled bleu cheese to biscuit dough and stir gently. Bake according to directions on box.

TOSSED SALAD

You might throw in thin slices of celery with some greens and toss with oil and garlic wine vinegar.

PINEAPPLE AVEDON

So named for its elegant simplicity:

2 cups fresh pineapple chunks   *1½ tablespoons brown sugar*
3 teaspoons granulated sugar   *⅓ cup sour cream*

Sprinkle pineapple with granulated sugar. Cover and chill. Beat brown sugar into sour cream until well blended. Top a serving of pineapple with the sour cream mixture and an added sprinkling of brown sugar. *Serves 2.*

The Man in the Gray Flannel Lederhosen

You married a bon vivant, a world traveler, a real live jet-setter. You have only two possible routes on your itinerary. Either clip his wings and ground that man quickly or leave the poor guy alone with his wanderlust. If he still likes to travel, let him. You married him because he was exciting, didn't you? Far better to treat him gently and make home his favorite port of call than to have him cancel out some day. We're not suggesting that you fill his two-suiter with melty chocolate chip cookies to remind him of the little woman, but do all you can to make him *want* to stay down on the farm.

Think for a minute—any longer is discouraging and downright demoralizing—about those winsome stewardesses he meets on each new jaunt. Aren't they all honey blond, dimpled and fairly dripping with Southern accents? And don't they leap to each pointless call of the male passengers while the poor females parch for a mere glass of water? They're not so dumb. They know that if dinner is a little late, all they need do is smile and offer him another cocktail. And he just laps it up.

So when he comes home wearing a smirk and a shiny new pair of Junior Pilot's wings, you know he's been acting like a kid again. This is the time to launch into action. Don that sari he brought from Bombay and serve up a succulent plate of Shrimp Sumatra. The world may be his oyster, but it's up to you to prepare it. And with this dinner under his peripatetic belt, he may very well realize the wisdom of flying family plan from now on.

SHRIMP SUMATRA

CRUSTY GARLIC BREAD   SPRING SALAD
DE GAULLE'S GÂTEAU

CHABLIS LES CLOS

SHRIMP SUMATRA

2½ *dozen large shrimp,*   ¼ *cup sliced green onions*
 shelled and deveined   *Salt and pepper to taste*
3 *tablespoons butter or more*   ¼ *cup dry white wine*
1 *cup sliced fresh mushrooms*

Sauté the shrimp in the butter over medium heat for 5 minutes. Add the mushrooms and onions and salt and pepper. Cook slowly until the shrimp turn pink, about 3 minutes. Add wine. Simmer and stir reverently for just 2 more minutes. *Serves 2.*

CRUSTY GARLIC BREAD

2 medium-sized French rolls
⅛ teaspoon garlic powder
Butter, softened

Split rolls. Mix garlic powder with some softened butter and smear on cut side of rolls. (*) Pop into a 375 degree oven when you start the shrimp and they'll be ready to accompany each other to the table. *Serves 2.*

SPRING SALAD

Pinch each garlic powder and
  oregano
½ jar marinated artichoke
  hearts
½ head romaine lettuce

½ head French endive
⅓ head cauliflower, broken
  into flowerets
1 tomato, cut into wedges
10 pitted ripe olives

Add garlic powder and oregano to marinated artichoke hearts. Let stand for several hours. Arrange romaine and endive leaves on two salad plates. Place artichokes, cauliflower, tomato wedges and olives on leaves. Drizzle with remaining marinade from the jar. *Serves 2.*

DE GAULLE'S GÂTEAU

1 pound cake
Peach preserves, raspberry preserves or orange marmalade
Cream sherry

Slice cake horizontally so that you have about 4 sections of ½ inch each. Spread the bottom three generously with the preserves, smearing it clear to the edges. Top with the fourth slice and secure with a few strategically located toothpicks. Sprinkle with 5–6 tablespoons cream sherry and bake at 350 degrees for 25 minutes. Remove from the oven and chill for 2 hours. Slice very thin and serve with very strong coffee. *Serves 8.*

Man with a Million

With the tax collector hard at our heels every time we've scraped together enough for a shampoo and set, it's hard for us to believe that millionaires haven't passed into extinction like the whooping crane and the great auk. But if we are to believe *Fortune* and *Business Week*, there must be enough millionaires floating around free to put visions of sugarplums in any girl's head.

If we had been among those who snagged one of these prizes, we'd now be able to look forward to the dinner hour with some enthusiasm, instead of the dead-heat panic that now overtakes us as the sun begins to sink behind the utility yard. Had we married Midases we would simply waft into the dining salon of our eighteenth century *châteaux,* trailing chiffon by Dior, and settle down to truffle-studded pheasant and Dom Perignon. Unfortunately we didn't and we don't.

Even if you did marry that millionaire, you must occasionally face the cruel fates that attend the rest of us every day. But at least your Judgment Day comes only once a week, on cook's night out. So here, in the spirit of charitable sharing, we offer a menu to tide you and your millionaire over those nights when you're roughing it without the old family retainers.

BLUE CHIP CHICKEN IN CHAMPAGNE

WILD RICE

ARTICHOKE HEARTS IN CHIVE SAUCE

LONG GREEN TORTE

CHAMPAGNE

BLUE CHIP CHICKEN IN CHAMPAGNE

2 chicken breasts

¼ cup butter

½ teaspoon salt

Dash pepper

½ cup dry champagne

⅓ cup white port

¼ cup brandy

1½ cups light cream

1 can cream sauce or:

CREAM SAUCE:

3 tablespoons butter

3 tablespoons flour

1 cup milk

Pat the chicken breasts tenderly with a paper towel until dry. Melt the butter in your heaviest skillet and while it melts sprinkle the chicken with salt and pepper. Sauté the chicken until it is tawny and crisp. Pop on a lid and cook, covered, over medium heat for 25 minutes or as long as it takes you to read the financial page. Of course if you haven't had the foresight to buy canned cream sauce, you will have to spend all that precious time making your own. If such is the case, melt the butter in a small saucepan, remove from the heat and stir in the flour to make a smooth paste. Return to the heat, gradually stir in the milk and simmer for 1 minute or until thickened.

Now back to that chicken, which by now should be tender and juicy. Remove the chicken from the skillet and discard the drippings. Add the champagne, port and brandy to the skillet; bring to boiling. Reduce the heat and simmer the spirits, uncovered, for 5 minutes. Now slip the light cream and cream sauce into the pan —don't even think of the calories or you'll stop right now—and stir until smooth. Cook for 5 minutes, stirring all the while. Return the chicken to its proper home, nestled in all that good sauce, and serve on a platter surrounded by wild rice. *Serves 2.*

WILD RICE

We have a feeling that some nice man probably spent years of his life perfecting packaged wild rice and we see no reason to try to improve upon his work. So open one of those handy packages and follow its easy directions.

ARTICHOKE HEARTS IN CHIVE SAUCE

1 package frozen artichoke
*   hearts*
3 tablespoons butter

2 teaspoons lemon juice
2 teaspoons chopped chives

Cook artichoke hearts according to the directions on the package. While you are melting the butter, drain the artichoke hearts. Add lemon juice to the butter and pour mixture over the hearts. Just before serving sprinkle with chopped chives. *Serves 4.*

LONG GREEN TORTE

2½ cups whole marshmal-
*   lows, firmly packed*
1¼ cups half and half
½ cup green crème de menthe
⅓ cup white crème de cacao
Green food coloring

1 cup crushed chocolate
*   wafer crumbs*
2 tablespoons melted butter
2 egg whites
3 tablespoons sugar
1½ cups heavy cream,
*   whipped*

Melt marshmallows with the half and half in a small pan. When melted set the pan in cold water and stir until mixture is cooled. Blend in the crème de menthe, crème de cacao and about 6 drops food coloring. Chill this mixture until it begins to thicken.

Mix chocolate crumbs and butter and pat evenly over the bottom of an 8- or 9-inch pan with removable bottom or spring form mold. Beat the egg whites until stiff and add sugar gradually while you are beating until the whites hold perky, short peaks. Thoroughly fold the marshmallow mixture and whites into the whipped cream. Pour into the pan lined with chocolate crust. Cover and freeze until firm (this should take about 8 hours). *Serves 12.*

Gallant Gourmet

A girl we know married a gallant gourmet and immediately retired from the kitchen. She figured that any man whose palate reveled in the likes of *Coq au Vin* was not going to be overwhelmed by her single culinary triumph over macaroni and cheese.

Besides, a true gourmet can easily be coerced into taking up the wooden spoon himself if you ply him with platitudes about men being the most creative chefs and keep the larder stocked with pounds of butter and bushels of fresh mushrooms. Of course once you've relinquished your authority over the kitchen you might as well forget any thoughts of a food budget; a man can pluck a supermarket's shelves clean before you've even dug your list out of the dark reaches of your purse.

So if you've married a Gallant Gourmet, all you have to do is provide the ingredients for this menu, leave the book propped open in some conspicuous place and sneak quietly out the back door. If your gourmet is truly gallant he will take care of the rest.

MEDALLIONS OF BEEF

SPINACH AND OYSTER CASSEROLE ROCKEFELLER

GARLIC POPOVERS

COEUR À LA CRÈME

LANCERS

MEDALLIONS OF BEEF

6 slices filet of beef	½ cup fresh mushrooms,
2 tablespoons olive oil	sliced
2 tablespoons flour	3 tablespoons chopped chives
1 cup consommé	Butter

Sauté the beef in olive oil for 2 minutes. Remove the meat and add flour to olive oil and brown, adding consommé until it becomes a rich brown sauce. Add the mushrooms and chives, which you have lightly sautéed in butter, and return the meat to the pan. Cook for another minute. *Serves 2.*

SPINACH AND OYSTER CASSEROLE ROCKEFELLER

*½ package frozen spinach
  soufflé
½ can frozen oysters
1 tablespoon butter
½ tablespoon minced onion
1 tablespoon minced celery*

*Pinch thyme
½ teaspoon Pernod
3 tablespoons fine dry bread
  crumbs
Butter*

Defrost the spinach soufflé and the oysters. Wash oysters and pat with a paper towel until dry. Melt butter and sauté the onion and celery until clear. Add onion and celery mixture, along with the thyme, Pernod and oysters to the spinach, being careful to distribute the oysters evenly throughout the mixture. Place in a casserole dish and top with bread crumbs. Dot with butter and bake in a 350 degree oven for 30 minutes and serve immediately. *Serves 2.*

GARLIC POPOVERS

Make Enormous Popover recipe (see Index), adding 1 teaspoon of garlic powder to the batter before baking.

Some gourmet shops carry popover mixes, and if you can find this it is quite good and almost foolproof. Just add the garlic powder and your Gallant Gourmet will think you've been slipping off to France for lessons at the Cordon Bleu.

COEUR À LA CRÈME

*1 8-ounce package cream
  cheese
⅛ cup heavy cream*

*1 tablespoon confectioners'
  sugar
1 box fresh strawberries
Unsalted crackers*

Line a small mold with cheesecloth. In a medium bowl beat cream cheese until light and fluffy. Gradually add cream and beat until smooth. Add sugar and mix thoroughly. Pack cream cheese mixture firmly into the mold. Cover with waxed paper and refrigerate overnight. Just before serving wash and drain the strawberries, but don't hull them. Unmold Coeur à la Crème onto a pretty serving plate. Surround with plump strawberries and crisp crackers. *Serves 2.*

Amorous Athlete

We have a friend who threatens every year to break the leg of every member of the National Football League. She figures that's the only way she'll ever see her husband again. She's married to an Amorous Athlete.

If you're in the same fix you must be well aware of the symptoms. Every weekend two television sets and at least one transistor radio blare in a cacophony of football, baseball or basketball games. As if that isn't bad enough, we now have golf matches and programs devoted to recapping what your armchair quarterback has already vicariously thrilled to all afternoon. And, while the fun and games continue, the house must be shrouded in darkness. The merest hint of the sun will cause a glare on the TV screen and your man will peevishly trudge on down to his buddy Mac's, whose wife left him years ago. What's more, she ran off with a skinny advertising copywriter who didn't know the difference between a split-T and a T-bone. Old Mac didn't even miss her until the last game was over that Sunday night.

Of course you probably don't want to go quite that far, so you'd better learn to live your life season by season. And every once in a while, when your husband looks particularly peaked and appears to be courting rickets from sitting in the same chair all weekend, pack a lunch and get him out in the fresh air. Of course the only way to do that is to hie him off to some kind of sporting event. But don't do it too often or sure as Arnold Palmer's putts,

you'll get a season ticket to the Green Bay Packers' games for
your birthday.

FRANK'S POTATO CHOWDER
HE-MAN HEARTY SANDWICHES
CRISP RAW VEGETABLES
MIDDLE MUDDLE CAKE

FRANK'S POTATO CHOWDER

½ cup diced onions
¼ cup finely diced celery
1 tablespoon butter
1 8-ounce can condensed
  chicken broth
½ teaspoon salt
Dash pepper

½ cup packaged sliced
  potatoes
¾ cup milk
¼ cup cream
1 teaspoon minced parsley
½ cup diced Cheddar cheese
2 frankfurters, sliced thin

Sauté onions and celery in butter until limp. Add chicken broth,
salt, pepper and potatoes. Cover and bring to a boil. Reduce heat
and simmer delicately until the potatoes are tender. Add milk,
cream, parsley and cheese. Heat just until cheese begins to ooze.
Meanwhile, brown frankfurters lightly in a skillet. Add to chowder
just before you place it in the thermos. *Serves 2.*

HE-MAN HEARTY SANDWICHES

½ cup sour cream
1 tablespoon dry onion soup
  mix

Softened butter or margarine
4 slices rye bread

1 teaspoon horseradish
¼ teaspoon salt
Dash pepper

6 slices cold roast beef
2 lettuce leaves

Mix the sour cream, onion soup mix, horseradish, salt and
pepper together. Spread butter on the bread and put 3 slices of
beef on 2 of the pieces of bread. Top with lettuce leaves and a

spoonful of the sour cream mixture. Cover with remaining slices of bread. He'll make a touchdown run to get one of these. *Serves 2.*

CRISP RAW VEGETABLES

Pack carrot sticks, celery and tiny cherry tomatoes in ice in an insulated bag. They will be crisp and tasty when you arrive at your destination. Don't forget a salt shaker.

MIDDLE MUDDLE CAKE

Put the frosting in the middle of this delicious chocolate cake to keep your fingers tidy while eating it.

⅔ cup chocolate bits
2 tablespoons rum or coffee
¼ pound (1 stick) softened
   butter
⅔ cup sugar
3 eggs, separated

⅓ cup ground almonds (you
   can do this in a blender)
¾ cup cake flour
¼ teaspoon almond extract
Pinch salt
2 tablespoons sugar

ICING:

½ cup chocolate bits
2 tablespoons coffee or rum
2–3 tablespoons soft butter

Melt chocolate bits and rum or coffee over hot (not boiling) water. Cream butter and sugar, add egg yolks, ground almonds, flour, almond extract and chocolate bit mixture. Beat egg whites until frothy, add a pinch of salt. When eggs are beginning to stiffen, add 2 tablespoons sugar and beat until very stiff. Add ⅓ of the egg whites to batter to soften it, then fold in the remainder. Pour into a greased 8-inch pan and bake at 350 degrees for 20–25 minutes. Cool 10 minutes—turn out on rack. Cake should be slightly shaky in the middle, so do not overbake. To make icing melt chocolate and coffee or rum over hot water. Add butter, a tablespoon at a time. Beat until fairly thick. Slice cake through the middle to make 2 layers and place the icing on the bottom layer, covering it with the top layer. This is not a high cake, but is very rich and will feed 8 hungry quarterbacks.

The Man with a Method

Actors can be moody creatures whose highs and lows are charted by the vernal equinox, the turning of the tides or some other occult influence undecipherable to us mere mortals. If you somehow wound up with an actor for a husband, you probably have already learned to live with the constant uncertainty that each new role brings. On any given evening he might be Othello or Sammy Glick, depending entirely on the vagaries of the casting director. So you, too, must learn to shift your role to suit his mood. If he is momentarily Macbeth, he's not likely to warm to your Constance MacKenzie.

Actors, more than any other group of men, put their egos squarely on the line every day. Thus they are a bit more sensitive when a new blow hits them in the same old bruise. If the show closes in Philly or his reviews read like an obituary, you'd better be there to cosset and tranquillize him. It's not a bad idea to have something delectable in the oven—he'll swear he couldn't choke it down, but once this meal is in the spotlight he'll immediately start asking for reruns.

THE BARD'S BEEFSTEAK PIE

BAKED TOMATOES

OFF-BROADWAY BEANS

APRICOT MOUSSE

BURGUNDY

THE BARD'S BEEFSTEAK PIE

EGG PASTRY:

1½ cups flour
½ teaspoon salt
½ cup butter

1 egg, slightly beaten
4–5 tablespoons milk

2½ pounds top sirloin, cut
into 1½-inch cubes
2½ teaspoons salt
¼ teaspoon pepper
1 teaspoon fines herbes
(don't let this intimidate
you; just combine a bit of
thyme, oregano, sage, rose-
mary, marjoram and basil)

6 tablespoons flour
1 pound mushrooms, sliced
4 tablespoons butter
¼ cup dry red wine
1 beaten egg

For the pastry, mix flour, salt and butter until the combination resembles fine crumbs. Add the egg and milk and mix until dough holds together in a ball. Chill.

Coat the meat cubes in a mixture of salt, pepper, herbs and flour. Brown the mushrooms in butter and remove from the pan. Add meat to the pan in which the mushrooms were sautéed and brown. Alternate layers of meat and mushrooms in a 2-quart casserole, starting with the meat and ending with an even layer of mushrooms. Pour the red wine over all.

Roll the chilled pastry on a generously floured board to make a round about ½ inch thick and large enough to fit the top of the casserole. Moisten the edges of the casserole and press the edge of the pastry round onto the rim. Flute the edges of the pastry cover and brush with beaten egg. Bake at 350 degrees for an hour. If the top of the pie begins to brown too quickly, cover with foil for the rest of the baking period. Serves 6 but if there are only 2 of you the leftovers are good. We're sure that if Shakespeare had tasted this fragrant pie he would have composed a sonnet in its honor.

BAKED TOMATOES

3 medium tomatoes
¾ teaspoon mustard
1 tablespoon minced onion
1½ teaspoons Worcestershire

Salt and pepper
4 tablespoons buttered bread
  crumbs
½ teaspoon dried basil

Wash the tomatoes and cut out the stems. Halve them cross-wise and arrange the slices with the cut side up in a baking pan. Spread with mustard and onion and drizzle the Worcestershire over the top. Sprinkle with salt and pepper; top with bread crumbs and basil. Bake, uncovered, in a 350 degree oven for 40 minutes. *Serves 6.*

OFF-BROADWAY BEANS

2 packages frozen green beans
  (*not French cut*)
1 teaspoon instant onion
½ cup olive oil
¼ cup wine vinegar

1 teaspoon salt
¼ teaspoon pepper
½ cup grated Parmesan
  cheese

Cook beans according to package directions. Drain, cool and toss with the remaining ingredients. Serve well chilled. *Serves 6.*

APRICOT MOUSSE

8 ounces dried apricots
1½ cups water
1 cup confectioners' sugar
1 teaspoon vanilla
2 cups whipped cottage
  cheese

1 cup heavy cream, whipped
Confectioners' sugar
Vanilla
Kirsch or Cointreau

Soak apricots 4 or 5 hours in the water. Cook in that same water until tender, adding a little more if needed, but leaving no excess when done. Add sugar and vanilla and cook, stirring constantly, until well blended and thick. Put through coarse sieve or food mill. Cool. Add whipped cottage cheese. Chill until ready to serve. Whip cream and add sugar, vanilla and kirsch or Cointreau to taste. Garnish with a plop of whipped cream. *Serves 6.*

Old Charlie

When the great love of your life dropped you for that curvy dimwit in the typing pool, who was there to dry your eyes and puff up your pride—Old Charlie, of course. And, even though you'd known him since you were both seven, it wasn't until then that you noticed his really sterling qualities.

Old Charlies are like that. They stand steadfastly by while you fall in and out of love a dozen times, biding their time until you've had your fill of the glory boys. Then they move in with their heavy artillery when your defenses are down.

The wonderful thing about marrying an Old Charlie is that he is something like a Whitman's Sampler—in him you get a bit of all men. Comfortable as a well-worn Mukluk, an Old Charlie often turns out to be a secret swinger. While he may yawn after one Gibson and prune roses for a hobby, Charlies sometimes do surprisingly rakish things. Just when you're conditioned to his tweeds and leather patches, he'll come home with a double-breasted blazer and a gross of paisley shirts. And what could be more out of character than Old Charlie in silk pajamas—yet there he stands, a bashful Hugh Heffner.

Since you didn't have to court Charlie with culinary master-pieces, he won't be spoiled and will be perfectly content to sup again on meat loaf seasoned with the shadow of your smile.

MOTHER MC CREE'S MEAT LOAF

or

MAMA MIA'S MEAT LOAF

or

ANOTHER MOTHER'S MEAT LOAF

GARLIC PUFFS

TANGY BROCCOLI

GINGERBREAD TORTE

CLARET

MOTHER McCREE'S MEAT LOAF

1½ pounds ground beef
¼ cup dry red wine
1 egg, beaten
¼ cup water
½ cup bread crumbs
¼ teaspoon sage
¼ teaspoon ground thyme
¼ teaspoon garlic powder

1 small onion, diced
2 tablespoons diced green
  pepper
1 teaspoon salt
1 cup shredded Cheddar
  cheese
1 cup sliced mushrooms

Combine the meat, wine, egg, water, crumbs, sage, thyme, garlic powder, onion, green pepper and salt. Mix together lightly. Turn the meat mixture onto a square of waxed paper and pat into a 12-inch square. Sprinkle cheese and mushrooms over meat; then roll like a jelly roll using the waxed paper to start the roll. Place the roll, seam side down, on a rack in a shallow pan. Bake at 350 degrees for 1½ hours. *Serves 6–8.*

MAMA MIA'S MEAT LOAF

1 pound ground beef
1 cup soft bread crumbs
3 eggs
½ cup grated Romano or
  Parmesan cheese
1 tablespoon instant onion
¼ cup water

1¼ teaspoons basil
1¾ teaspoons salt
¼ teaspoon pepper
1 tablespoon olive oil
2 tablespoons fine bread
  crumbs
½ pound ricotta cheese

Mix meat, bread crumbs, 2 eggs, cheese, onion, water, 1 teaspoon basil, 1½ teaspoons salt and pepper. Brush the inside of a 9×5-inch loaf pan with the olive oil and sprinkle with fine bread crumbs. Pat half of the meat mixture into the pan. Mix the ricotta cheese with the remaining egg, ¼ teaspoon basil and ¼ teaspoon salt. Spread the mixture over the meat. Place the rest of the meat on top of the cheese. Bake in a 350 degree oven for 1 hour. *Serves 6.*

ANOTHER MOTHER'S MEAT LOAF

1 cup sliced fresh mushrooms
½ cup chopped onion
2 tablespoons butter or
margarine
⅓ cup sour cream
2 eggs

⅔ cup milk
1½ pounds ground round
¾ cup soft bread crumbs
2 teaspoons salt
1 teaspoon Worcestershire

Sauté the mushrooms and onion in butter. Remove from heat and stir in the sour cream. Combine the remaining ingredients and shape half of this mixture into an oval in a shallow baking pan. Now dig a little well in the middle for the filling; spoon the sour cream mixture into this indentation. Shape the rest of the meat over the filling, making sure all of the filling is covered. Seal the meat loaf well around the edges. Bake at 350 degrees for 1 hour. Let stand 15 minutes before slicing. *Serves 6.*

GARLIC PUFFS

1 package hot-roll mix
1 clove garlic, crushed
1 teaspoon coarse salt

1 egg
1 tablespoon water

Prepare the hot-roll mix following directions on the package. Let rise and then punch down and roll out into 4×16-inch oblong. Cut in half lengthwise; then cut each strip into 8 2-inch squares. Roll each square into a ball and place in a well-greased muffin cup. Mix crushed garlic clove with the salt. Beat the egg with water and brush the top of each roll. Sprinkle garlic-salt mixture over tops of rolls. Let rise until double and place in a preheated 375 degree oven for 15–18 minutes. *Makes 16 puffs.*

TANGY BROCCOLI

1 package frozen broccoli
1 chicken bouillon cube
1 teaspoon instant onion
¼ teaspoon marjoram leaves

¼ teaspoon basil leaves
2 tablespoons melted butter
or margarine

Cook broccoli according to the package directions, adding the chicken bouillon cube to the cooking water. Drain broccoli and add onion, marjoram and basil. Dress with melted butter. *Serves 3.*

GINGERBREAD TORTE

1 package gingerbread mix   *½ cup chopped walnuts*
2 cups heavy cream   *1¼ teaspoons maple flavoring*
¼ cup confectioners' sugar

Make gingerbread according to package directions and bake in a 9×9-inch pan. Cool cake in pan for 10 minutes, remove from pan and cool completely on wire rack. While the cake is cooling, whip cream with confectioners' sugar until stiff. Remove 1¼ cups whipped cream to a small bowl, fold in walnuts and maple flavoring. Split cake to make 2 layers, then split again to make 4. Put layers together with the cream-nut mixture and frost top and sides with plain whipped cream. Sprinkle top with additional chopped nuts. Refrigerate 2 hours before serving and we suggest that a sturdy lock be placed on the refrigerator door during this period. *Serves 9.*

Rekindling the flame

2.

REKINDLING
THE
FLAME

Love doesn't grow on the trees like apples
in Eden—it's something you have to make.
And you must use your imagination to make
it too, just like anything else. It's all
work, work.

JOYCE CARY

These days a new bride hardly has time to shake the rice out of her peignoir before being inundated with advice about how to "keep the magic in marriage." Since we don't want to be caught poaching on the experts' territory, we'll merely add our own few words of advice and move smartly on to some recipes which should keep him so charmed that he'll think you're a descendant of Circe.

It has been our experience that the magic begins to dwindle noticeably the day he catches you doing your thigh slap exercises, or when it's time to take the garbage out. At these junctures neither mink eyelashes nor vinyl miniskirts are going to rekindle his interest.

If, however, things are looking generally grim for no apparent reason, it may be time to take steps to revive your sagging existence. There is no cure-all for a mid-season slump, but often as not, the culprit is just the boredom of habit. Balzac had the key when he said, "Marriage should combat without respite or mercy that monster which devours everything—habit."

Take weekends, for instance. If you've been using them as wastebaskets for the week's work, quit it. Work like a demon during the week if you must, but save those two precious days for trips to the zoo, picnics at the beach, dancing under the stars or lying in a hammock.

One evening turn off the television set and talk to each other. Or take up chess together, or cribbage, or buy a Ouija board. Get some Broadway show albums and listen to them together. Share a midnight supper for two after the tots have been smuggled off to bed; serve cheese, fruit, French bread and wine. Go to a movie and share a box of popcorn. Close your drapes and try out the new dances in your own living room. Study Italian together from a language record—Italian is the language of love. Divvy up the Sunday newspaper and share your ideas about the world. Save your pennies to buy a painting and then spend your Saturday afternoons scouring the galleries for the one you love.

Another good place to begin your assault on habit is at the breakfast table. During the week most men start the day with a gulp of coffee, a vitamin pill and a frantic dash for the 8:10. We think that's just great. For contrary to what you have been led to believe, most men don't want you puttering around them in the morning, frying bacon in your cheerful pink chintz. They'd much rather snarl and snap over the editorial page in solitary splendor.

Yet somehow the people who package breakfast foods have managed to perpetuate the myth that no man should be sent off to the wars without having his drowsy digestive tract assaulted by a gargantuan meal. Don't you believe it. For one thing, most men feel obligated to rush for the doughnuts at 10:00 and if they are already bloated with eggs and bacon and hot mush, they will be hard pressed to hold their own at the caterer's wagon.

When you are bent on baiting his interest don't waste your time or temper on weekday breakfasts. Save up your energy for those few alluring and romantic mornings when you have plenty of time to enjoy each other's company.

Even though you may not be the type who sparkles in the morning (and we suspect that even Twiggy looks better after her coffee), do your best to get your eyebrows, mouth and eyelashes all on in their proper places. It's disconcerting for a man to find himself seated across the table from a boiled egg wearing a housecoat.

Good food and your ravishing face alone should start his anti-freeze functioning, but there are some additional refinements you can employ. If he is a current events fanatic and you are holed up in the hinterlands—beg, borrow or steal a copy of the Sunday edition of the New York *Times*. Even if it's a week old he'll love it. If he's a word wizard be sure to have a dictionary at your elbow and share the Sunday crossword. But if you have the extraordinary bad luck of choosing a day when there is a football, baseball and/or basketball game gracing your television set, grit your teeth and try to enjoy it. For the most beautiful breakfast in the world turns to ashes in the mouth of a man who has just missed a grand slam home run.

ORANGE JUICE WITH MINT LEAVES

DOWN UNDER TOAST

or

HITCHING POST TOAST

or

EVE'S TOAST

BACON

COFFEE

ORANGE JUICE WITH MINT LEAVES

Simply decorate each glass of orange juice with fresh sprigs of mint.

DOWN UNDER TOAST

1 egg, beaten   *Oil*
⅓ cup milk   *¼ cup apple butter*
¼ teaspoon salt   *Powdered sugar*
4 slices raisin nut bread

Combine the egg, milk and salt in a shallow pie pan and beat with a fork. Dip each bread slice into the egg mixture, turning to coat both sides. Grill or pan fry bread in hot oil. Spread 2 table-spoons of apple butter on 2 slices of the toast and cover with the remaining slices. Sprinkle with powdered sugar. *Serves 2 and can easily be doubled to serve 4.*

HITCHING POST TOAST

2 tablespoons butter
¼ cup brown sugar
¼ cup crushed pineapple,
    drained

1 egg
¾ cup milk
Pinch salt
4 slices white bread

Set your oven at 400 degrees. Melt the butter in a 9-inch-square baking pan and stir sugar and crushed pineapple into the butter. Spread this mixture over the bottom of the pan. Beat the egg, milk and salt together in a bowl and soak the bread in this combi-nation until it's soft; then place over the pineapple and brown sugar mixture in the pan. Bake for 25 minutes, or until golden brown. Cool for a moment and then invert on a heated serving plate. *Serves 2.*

EVE'S TOAST

3 medium oranges
⅛ cup honey
1 egg
¼ teaspoon salt

1 teaspoon sugar
¼ cup orange juice
¼ cup milk
4 slices bread

Peel the oranges and cut into bite-size pieces. Stir honey into the orange pieces and set aside. Beat the egg slightly and add salt, sugar, orange juice and milk. Dip the bread slices in the egg mixture and brown both sides on a well-greased griddle. Serve with a topping of the sweetened orange pieces. *Serves 2 or double for 4 (amount of salt remains the same).*

BROILED BANANAS
THE CHICKEN AND THE EGG
SAUSAGE PATTIES WITH GRILLED TOMATOES

COFFEE

This is a very hearty menu and makes a good filling brunch even when you won't be eating dinner until late in the evening.

BROILED BANANAS

2 bananas
2 tablespoons melted butter
3 tablespoons sugar

Split the bananas and dip in the melted butter. Dust with sugar and place on a broiler pan. Broil about 6 inches from the heat, turning once. *Serves 4.*

THE CHICKEN AND THE EGG

1 cup cream sauce   *Salt to taste*
½ cup minced cooked chicken *2 eggs*
¼ cup toasted slivered
*   almonds*

Combine the cream sauce with the chicken and almonds and salt to your taste. Divide the mixture between 2 individual casseroles and top each with an egg. Cook in a 350 degree oven for 20 minutes or until the eggs are done as you like them. *Serves 2.*

SAUSAGE PATTIES WITH GRILLED TOMATOES

1 large firm tomato   *Bread crumbs*
½ pound bulk sausage meat   *Parmesan cheese*
Salt and pepper

Slice the tomatoes ½ inch thick. Form the sausage into 2 patties and broil on one side. Turn and put the tomatoes on top. Sprinkle with salt and pepper. Add bread crumbs and a dash of cheese.

Drizzle on a bit of the sausage fat and continue broiling until the tomatoes are well browned. *Serves 4.*

APPLE POLISHERS' BAKED APPLES

HAM AND EGG SANDWICH

COFFEE

APPLE POLISHERS' BAKED APPLES

2 apples	*1 teaspoon grated lemon rind*
2 tablespoons raisins	*2 tablespoons sugar*
1 wineglass white wine	*1 tablespoon butter*
(6 ounces)	

Core the apples. Soak raisins in wine for ½ hour. Drain. Combine raisins, lemon rind and sugar and stuff the centers of the apples with the mixture. Dot with butter and moisten with the wine in which the raisins were soaked. Bake at 375 degrees for 1 hour. *Serves 2.*

HAM AND EGG SANDWICH

(make them the night before)

6 slices sourdough French bread	*2 tablespoons horseradish mustard*
2 tablespoons soft butter	*2 eggs*
1 slice ham	*2 cups milk*
	½ teaspoon Worcestershire

Spread each piece of bread with butter. Trim the ham of any fat and then dice into ¼-inch cubes. Combine the ham with mustard and mix well. Spread the ham mixture over 3 slices of bread and cover with the remaining slices. Arrange the sandwiches snugly in a small baking dish (you may have to trim them to fit).

Beat eggs slightly and stir in milk and Worcestershire. Pour this egg mixture over the sandwiches and let them stand covered overnight in the refrigerator. (*) Bake at 350 degrees for 1 hour and 20 minutes, or until custard is set. *Serves 2. (2 for him, 1 for you).*

FRESH STRAWBERRIES

EGGS SARAH JACKMAN

COFFEE

FRESH STRAWBERRIES

1 box strawberries
½ cup sour cream
¼ cup brown sugar

Select sweet fat beauties, then bring them gently home. Wash them lightly and drain. Serve, complete with hulls, along with a bowl of tart sour cream and a dish of sweet brown sugar for dipping. *Serves 2.*

EGGS SARAH JACKMAN

2 bagels
8 slices lox

HOLLANDAISE:

4 egg yolks   *½ teaspoon salt*
2 tablespoons lemon juice *½ cup melted butter*

Split the bagels and toast them. Meanwhile place the egg yolks, lemon juice and salt in your blender jar. Turn on and off very quickly. Heat butter until it is bubbly. Turn the blender on high and dribble the butter into the whirring egg mixture steadily until the mixture emulsifies and thickens. Place 2 slices of lox on each half of the toasted bagels. Cover with hollandaise and serve. *Serves 2.*

NECTARINES OF THE GODS
KNOCK-OUT TROUT
TOASTED FRENCH BREAD
MARMALADE
COFFEE

NECTARINES OF THE GODS

3–4 nectarines

2 tablespoons butter or margarine

2 tablespoons brown sugar

Lemon juice

Slice but do not peel the nectarines. Heat the butter or margarine and brown sugar in a skillet until bubbling. Add the nectarines and cook until glazed and shiny. Sprinkle with lemon juice and serve hot. *Serves 2.*

KNOCK-OUT TROUT

2 tablespoons butter

1 tablespoon oil

2 trout

2 tablespoons flour

1 tablespoon chopped parsley

2 tablespoons toasted slivered almonds

Salt and pepper

Lemon

Melt the butter and the oil in a heavy skillet. Dust the trout well with flour. Sauté the fish gently, turning several times until the fish is cooked just through, but not overdone. The fish should be moist but still easily flaked with a fork. Sprinkle with chopped parsley, toasted slivered almonds and dust with salt and pepper. Garnish with lemon wedges. *Serves 2.*

Nooners

We know how easy it is to slip unconsciously into the old sandwich and potato chip routine for lunch and there's certainly nothing wrong with that on weekends when the north forty has to be plowed, but once in a while it's worth the trouble to make lunch a pleasant idyll.

This is a good time to give your patio or terrace a workout. Set the table with something more festive than paper plates and then be sure the table doesn't outshine you—old Levis and a paint-spattered shirt won't do. Wear something flattering and feminine and when he sees you sitting across from him exuding elegance and polish he will be so staggered he'll probably decide that you were meant for a life of luxury. Don't be surprised if he suddenly sells the house, quits his job and whisks you off to the Greek islands to spend your days drinking Retsina, dancing barefoot on the Acropolis and sailing the Aegean Sea.

NEVER ON SUNDAY SALAD

GREEK BREAD

FROSTY GRAPES

ICED RUM COFFEE

or

CHILLED CHABLIS

NEVER ON SUNDAY SALAD

You can have it on Sunday, but if you can convince him to come home for lunch during the week so much the better.

½ *head lettuce*
1 chopped green onion
½ *cucumber, peeled and sliced*
1 tomato, peeled and cut into wedges

½ *green pepper, diced*
3 anchovies, chopped
1 tablespoon minced parsley
¼ *cup Greek olives (or salty Italian)*
½ *cup cubed feta cheese*

DRESSING:

¾ *cup olive oil*
½ *cup cider vinegar*
1 small clove garlic, minced

1 teaspoon dry mustard
½ *teaspoon salt*
⅛ *teaspoon pepper*

Rip the lettuce into small pieces and place in your favorite salad bowl. Add the onion, cucumber, tomatoes, green pepper, anchovies, parsley, olives and cheese. In a jar mix the oil, vinegar, garlic, mustard and salt and pepper. Shake the dressing well and pour just enough over the salad to film each leaf. Save the rest for another salad. *Serves 2.*

GREEK BREAD

1 tablespoon dill weed
1 loaf frozen white bread
  dough, defrosted

2 tablespoons butter or
  margarine
Yellow cornmeal

Add the dill weed to the defrosted bread dough and push and pummel the dough mercilessly until it is thoroughly mixed in. Grease 3 individual (4½×2½×1½ inches) loaf pans. Divide the dough into three pieces and place in the pans. Cover the pans with towels and let the dough rise in a warm place until it plumps up nicely above the pans. Now brush the tops of the loaves with the melted butter and sprinkle them lightly with cornmeal. Bake for 20 minutes at 400 degrees or until the loaves sound like Shelley Manne's drums when tapped with your fingertips.

Remove the bread from the pans and cool slightly on wire racks. Serve warm. *Makes 3 individual loaves.*

FROSTY GRAPES

1 pound large sweet grapes
1 egg white, lightly beaten
Confectioners' sugar

Dip the stemmed grapes in egg white and roll in sugar. Arrange them in a pyramid on a dessert platter and chill until you are ready to serve. *Serves 2.*

ICED RUM COFFEE

For each serving, pour 1 ounce of dark rum over ice. Fill with cooled coffee. Top with whipped cream and serve. *Serves 2.*

The Shank of the Night

*"The loves of some people are
but the results of good suppers."*

NICOLAS CHAMFORT

When the chill winds begin to blow, anyone with an ounce of romance in his soul knows that a crackling fire warms more than the toes. So take advantage of a blustering evening to settle down in front of a cozy hearth with good food, good wine and a little music. You'll kindle your own blaze.

GAZPACHO

COSTA BRAVA PIE

HONEYED PEACHES

CLARET

GAZPACHO

This Spanish soup-salad wafts a bit of summer into winter's gray days.

*1 cup finely chopped peeled
tomato*
*½ cup finely chopped green
pepper*
*½ cup peeled, finely chopped
cucumber*
¼ cup finely chopped onion
2 teaspoons snipped parsley
1 teaspoon snipped chives

1 small clove garlic, minced
*3 tablespoons tarragon wine
vinegar*
2 tablespoons olive oil
1 teaspoon salt
*¼ teaspoon freshly ground
black pepper*
Tabasco sauce to taste
4 cups tomato juice

Combine all the ingredients in a steel or glass bowl. Cover and chill for 4 hours. Serves 6 easily, but the leftovers won't wilt and they make great diet lunches.

COSTA BRAVA PIE

Fresh mushrooms and cottage cheese rendezvous in a rich crust.

1½ pounds mushrooms,
cleaned and sliced
1 cup thinly sliced onions
4 tablespoons butter
⅓ cup flour
1 carton (8 ounces) small
curd cottage cheese

¼ cup parsley
¼ cup dry sherry
1 teaspoon salt
⅛ teaspoon black pepper
1 package piecrust mix

Set oven at 425 degrees. Sauté the mushrooms and onions in butter until glossy. Add the flour and mix well. Remove from heat. Toss in the cottage cheese, parsley, sherry, salt and pepper and mix thoroughly.

Prepare piecrust according to directions and roll half of it into a 12-inch circle. Line a 9-inch pie pan with the pastry, allowing the extra dough to flop over the edge. Roll out the remaining dough and cut into ½-inch strips. Pour filling into the pie pan and arrange the pastry strips in a lattice pattern on top of the filling. Tuck in the overhanging crust and flute it. This mysterious process, which apparently every woman is supposed to understand from birth, is not, as we once thought, some type of musical incantation. Fluting simply means to pinch the edge of the crust into neat little ridges. Bake on the bottom rack of the oven for 40–45 minutes. If the pie appears to be browning too fast after 20 minutes or so, cover the edge with a piece of foil. Cool for 5 minutes before serving. A Costa Brava pie will serve 6, so send the extra to your neighbors, but don't ask them to share your romantic fireside.

HONEYED PEACHES

4 tablespoons honey
3 tablespoons rum
2 large ripe peaches, peeled, stoned and sliced

Heat the honey and rum and pour over the peaches. *Serves 2.*

There are few things more romantic than an evening of music under the stars. So when summer rolls around don't waste any time—pack an elegant dinner in a basket, grab your man by the hand and head for the nearest outdoor concert. If your city isn't blessed with concerts in the park you can still enjoy all the benefits of open-air music. Stack your hi-fi with your favorite records, open a window and enjoy your sumptuous dinner and private musicale in the seclusion of your own back yard or terrace.

SANGRÍA
VAGABOND HAM AND VEAL PIE
CHERRY TOMATOES
RUM FUDGE BROWNIES
NECTARINES

SANGRIA

1 fifth dry red wine
Juice ½ lemon
Juice 1 orange

1 package frozen peaches
Soda
Ice

Combine the wine with the fruit juices and peaches. Let it stand until the peaches are defrosted. Pour into a tall pitcher or a thermos and add soda to taste. Serve chilled over ice. *Serves 4.*

VAGABOND HAM AND VEAL PIE

2 sticks piecrust mix
1 can (4½-ounce) deviled ham
1½ pounds veal cutlet
2 tablespoons chopped onion
2 tablespoons finely chopped parsley
Dash salt
¼ teaspoon marjoram leaves

¼ teaspoon thyme
Pepper
1 pound ham slice, fully cooked
4 hard-cooked eggs, sliced
1 egg, slightly beaten
1 cup chicken broth
1 envelope gelatin

Set oven at 350 degrees. Prepare the piecrust according to the directions on the package and shape into a ball. Remove about ⅓ of the pastry and set aside.

Roll out the larger blob of the pastry into a 12-inch circle (or ragged ellipse if you roll out pastry like we do) and place it in a deep fluted pie pan, letting the pastry stand up around the edge.

Spread the deviled ham over the pastry and arrange half of the veal over it. Combine the onion, parsley, salt, marjoram, thyme and pepper. Sprinkle on a layer of the herbs and add half of the ham. Arrange the egg slices on top and add one more layer of each of the veal, herbs and ham.

Roll out another circle of piecrust dough and place on top of the pie plate. Bring the edge of the bottom crust over the top crust and press the edges together and crimp as if you were giving a finger wave. Cut a round hole in the center of the top crust to let the steam out.

If you are artistically inclined, use any leftover dough to cut out decorative shapes and place on top of the crust. Brush with beaten egg and slip into the oven for 1½ hours.

About 15 minutes before the pie is done place the chicken broth in a small saucepan and sprinkle gelatin on top. Heat and stir until the gelatin is dissolved. Let the mixture stand at room temperature. After the pie has finished baking and has cooled for 30 minutes, pour the chicken broth mixture into the center of the pie. Let the pie cool for another 2 hours and then refrigerate. If you wish to carry the pie to an outdoor concert remove it from the refrigerator just before leaving and carry it in a cooler or an insulated bag. *Serves 6.*

RUM FUDGE BROWNIES

1 package brownie mix
1 egg
½ cup coarsely chopped
  walnuts

2 tablespoons light rum
¼ cup confectioners' sugar

Set oven at 350 degrees. Make the brownies according to the package directions, using the egg, walnuts and the amount of water indicated on the package. Pour into a 9×9-inch greased pan and bake for 30 minutes. Cool for 15 minutes and then pour rum over the warm brownies. When the brownies are cool, sift confectioners' sugar over the top. *Makes 16 brownies.*

———

In the crush of daily events husbands have occasionally been known to let an anniversary slip by unnoticed. You can, of course, drop hints lavishly during the preceding weeks, mark his calendar with a big red X, clue in his secretary and take all the usual precautions. But if your man tends to lapses of memory, protect your girlish illusions by planning your own celebration. Rather than wait breathlessly for that elusive dinner invitation, plot an anniversary dinner so splendid that next year will find you popping champagne corks in the honeymoon suite of the Fairmont in San Francisco.

CASANOVA'S CORNISH GAME HENS

ARTFUL ARTICHOKES

SPICED CRABAPPLE OR GREEN PEAR HALVES

PLUM FLAMBÉ

DRY SAUTERNE OR DRY WHITE GRAVES

CASANOVA'S CORNISH GAME HENS

DRESSING:

⅓ *cup onion, chopped*	*Dash paprika*
¼ *cup celery, chopped*	*1¾ cups diced stale bread*
2 tablespoons melted butter	*½ cup chopped pecans*
½ teaspoon salt	*⅛ cup chopped parsley*

BIRDS:

2 defrosted Cornish hens	*⅓ cup bouillon*
2 tablespoons melted butter	*¾ teaspoon cornstarch*
Salt	*1 tablespoon water*
Pepper	

Set the oven at 425 degrees. For the dressing sauté onions and celery in butter until glossy and limp. Add salt and paprika. Remove from heat and mix with the other dressing ingredients, using a delicate hand. Stuff the hens, securing the opening with toothpicks and tying the legs together. Place the hens in a roasting pan and douse with melted butter. Sprinkle with salt and pepper. Roast the hens at 425 degrees for 1–1¼ hours, basting occasionally with pan drippings. When the hens are crisp and golden brown remove them from the oven and glaze with hot bouillon thickened with cornstarch and water.

ARTFUL ARTICHOKES

8 frozen artichoke hearts	*Salt*
1 egg yolk	*Dill weed*
1 tablespoon lemon juice	

Cook artichokes as directed on the package. Meanwhile prepare the sauce: beat the egg yolk until creamy and slowly beat in the lemon juice. Drizzle in 1½ teaspoons of the hot liquid in which the artichokes are cooking. While you continue beating the sauce occasionally, drain the artichokes. Pour the sauce over the artichokes, sprinkle with salt and a touch of dill weed before serving. *Serves 2.*

PLUM FLAMBÉ

3 tablespoons sugar	*¼ teaspoon lemon peel*
4 tablespoons light corn syrup	*¾ teaspoon cornstarch*
¼ cup water	*2 cloves*
4 purple plums, pitted and quartered	*1½ tablespoons kirsch*
¾ teaspoon cold water	*½ pint vanilla ice cream*
¼ teaspoon lemon juice	*2 meringue shells*

Combine the sugar, corn syrup and water in a saucepan. Add the plums and bring to a boil. Cover and simmer for about 5 minutes or until the plums are soft. Remove the plums from the syrup and blend ¾ teaspoon water, the lemon juice and peel into the cornstarch. Stir until smooth and add to the syrup, beating constantly. Add the cloves and cook the sauce, stirring with a vengeance, until it is clear. Return the plums to the sauce and heat thoroughly. Place the plum mixture in a serving dish, pour heated kirsch over the sauce and ignite. Serve the flaming sauce over ice cream in the meringue shells. *Serves 2.*

Western men have long been fascinated by the shy, gentle women of the Orient. It's no wonder, really, that Japanese women are so desirable. A well-bred Japanese girl is trained from childhood in modesty and service. By the time she has reached the age of consent she will have mastered the arts of ikebana (flower arrangement), chanoyu (formal tea ceremony) and should be able to sew 100 stitches per minute.

However, even if your flower arrangements look like Phyllis Diller's hairdo, your tea ceremony consists of dropping a bag in hot water and the very thought of those hundred stitches makes you hug your Singer in gratitude, there's still a lot to be learned from the tender gender of Japan.

When your husband no longer lingers over his morning coffee just to gaze at your Ponds complexion and when late office meetings become the rule and not the exception, the time has come for a Geisha Dinner. The atmosphere for this dinner is nearly as important as the food. If you've never had a globe-trotting aunt to bring you a kimono from Japan, you'll just have to make do with a smashing hostess outfit. When your weary warrior comes home greet him with slippers, a steaming hot towel from which all of the water has been wrung and a tiny cup of exquisitely warming saki.

When he has relaxed and had time to consider at length his great good fortune in finding you, you may begin the final preparations for this Far Eastern feast.

SUKIYAKI
RICE
KUMQUAT PARFAIT
FORTUNE COOKIES

SAKI

SUKIYAKI

1 pound thinly sliced filet or sirloin tip

3 scallions, cut in 2-inch sections

¼ cup bean curd squares (Tofu)

2 onions, thinly sliced

3 ribs celery, sliced on the diagonal

1 cup thinly sliced mushrooms

½ pound spinach cut crosswise in 1-inch strips

1 cup bean sprouts or cooked drained Shirataki

¼ cup soy sauce

¼ cup chicken bouillon

1 teaspoon sugar

½ teaspoon MSG

2 tablespoons saki

1 strip beef suet or 1½ tablespoons cooking oil

A fling at Sukiyaki will give you a chance to browse through your local import grocery. The bean curd, bean sprouts and Shirataki (spaghetti-like yam shreds) are not absolutely necessary if you can't find them, but they do make the dish more interesting and certainly more authentic.

Arrange the meat, scallions, Tofu, onions, celery, mushrooms, spinach and bean sprouts or Shirataki on a large platter with all the care of a painter arranging a still life. The platter may be covered with plastic wrap and refrigerated at this point, but be sure to allow the ingredients to resume room temperature before cooking. Mix together the soy sauce, bouillon, sugar, MSG and saki and place in a small pitcher. This, too, can be refrigerated for later use.

When you are ready to begin the orderly ritual of preparing Sukiyaki, bring an electric skillet to the table and set it at a medium heat. Place the suet in the pan and when it has melted remove the unrendered* bits and add the beef slices. Cook the beef briefly; do not allow it to brown. Push the cooked meat to

* *when all the fat has cooked out and only the fiber is left*

the side and add the vegetables in sequence, beginning with the scallions. This is the time when you can really impress your guest of honor as you flash your chopsticks between platter and pan. Of course all you need to do is tilt the plate and give the vegetables a smart push in the right direction, but he will be so dazzled by your virtuosity that he won't even notice how simple it really is.

As the vegetables are added, slowly pour in the soy-broth mixture. This will steam the vegetables but will not overcook them. Mix the meat in with the vegetables and heat for about 4 additional minutes. The vegetables should remain crisp and colorful.

As an authentic (we think a bit *too* authentic) touch you may wish to place an unbeaten raw egg in a small dish. Each diner can then whip up the egg with his chopsticks and dip each bit of Sukiyaki into it. *Serves 4.*

RICE

If you want rice with all the good nutrients, follow the recipe on the rice box. But if you want to know why the rice in a Chinese or Japanese restaurant tastes so different and so good, try this.

1 cup long grain rice
Water

Wash the rice thoroughly (this is where the nutrition ladies would rap your knuckles) and drain. Put in a saucepan with water covering the rice by about ¾ inch. Bring the water to a boil and leave over a high heat for about 5 minutes. Stir it occasionally during this time to prevent sticking. When most of the water has boiled off cover the pan tightly and cook over a low heat for at least 20 minutes, or until the rice is tender and dry. When you lift the lid you will see one of the mysteries of the inscrutable Orient solved before your very eyes. *Serves 4.*

KUMQUAT PARFAIT

½ cup preserved kumquats   *¼ cup whipped cream*
¼ pint orange ice   *2 whole preserved kumquats*
¼ pint vanilla ice cream

Chop the kumquats coarsely. Layer the orange ice, half of the chopped kumquats, and the ice cream in 2 parfait glasses. Top with the other half of the kumquats and whipped cream. Garnish each parfait with a whole kumquat and serve chilled. *Serves 2.*

FORTUNE COOKIES

You can buy these in a grocery store or from your local Chinese restaurant. But you can make them special by removing the mass-produced fortunes and inserting some of your own creation. Use tweezers for this delicate operation. Of course you probably won't do this, and frankly neither would we.

SAKI

This Japanese rice wine resembles a dry sherry and is served warm in tiny thimble-like cups. It's easy to understand why, for saki contains a whopping 16 per cent alcohol. So serve it with discretion or you may find yourself with a slumbering samurai on your hands.

A Japanese couple, having finished a dinner like this, would repair to the bathhouse where they would enjoy each other's company and a good scrub in a steaming hot bath. It seems a shame that American bathtubs are built on such skimpy lines, but it's probably just as well or how would the dinner dishes ever get washed?

Some men are constitutionally unsuited to exotic dishes. Fondly known as "meat and potatoes men," they have never outgrown their native distrust of herbs and spices. If you happen to be stuck with a member of this reactionary breed don't try to ply him with Sukiyaki.

On the other hand, you don't have to forgo the pleasures of a Geisha Dinner entirely. The following menu will satisfy his carnivorous nature without upsetting his sensitive taste buds. If you can make it over the soy sauce hump you're home free.

BEEF AND MELON TERIYAKI
RICE
GREEN SALAD WITH BEAN SPROUTS
GRAPEFRUIT FRAPPÉ
CINNAMON PUFFS

BEER

BEEF AND MELON TERIYAKI

MARINADE:

¼ cup soy sauce
4 tablespoons sherry
1½ teaspoons sugar
1½ teaspoons oil
¼ teaspoon powdered ginger

1 tablespoon fresh ginger (if available)
1 clove garlic, crushed
1½ teaspoons cornstarch

1 pound top round, cut in ½-inch strips
1 tablespoon oil
½ small onion, sliced

½ green pepper, in strips
⅓ cup pineapple juice
1 package frozen melon balls

Combine all of the ingredients in the marinade except the cornstarch and place the meat in it for 1 hour. Brown the beef in oil and place in a baking dish. Add ¼ cup of the marinade and bake uncovered for 40 minutes at 325 degrees. While the meat is roasting, add the onion, pepper and pineapple juice to the browning skillet. Cook for about 10 minutes. Mix the cornstarch with the remaining marinade and add to the pineapple juice mixture. Cook until thick and glossy. Remove from the heat until the meat has finished cooking. When the meat is ready, bring the marinade to a boil. add the melon balls and heat for 5 minutes. Pour sauce over beef and serve immediately. *Serves 2.*

RICE

(See Index)

GREEN SALAD WITH BEAN SPROUTS

Toss your favorite green salad together, but just before adding the dressing throw in a handful of fresh or well-drained canned bean sprouts.

GRAPEFRUIT FRAPPÉ

1 envelope unflavored gelatin	1 tablespoon lemon juice
¼ cup cold water	1 12-ounce can frozen grape-
1 8-ounce can chilled crushed	fruit juice concentrate
pineapple	2 cups crushed ice

Soften the gelatin in the water and heat until the gelatin melts. Pour the pineapple with its syrup into the blender and blend until smooth. Add gelatin to the pineapple and blend again. Pour in the lemon juice, grapefruit juice and crushed ice. Blend thoroughly. Pour the mixture into parfait glasses and serve garnished prettily with mint leaves. *Serves 6.*

CINNAMON PUFFS

2 cups sifted flour	1 teaspoon grated orange
1 teaspoon baking powder	rind
1 cup sugar	1 cup chocolate chips
3 teaspoons cinnamon	½ cup nuts
½ cup softened butter or	1 egg white
margarine	⅔ cup sugar
½ cup soft shortening	2 teaspoons cinnamon
1 egg yolk	

Sift together the dry ingredients and add butter, shortening, egg yolk and shredded orange rind. Mix well. Add the chocolate chips, nuts and mix thoroughly. Shape the dough into 1-inch balls and dip into slightly beaten egg white. Roll each in sugar and cinnamon mixture. Place on a greased cookie sheet and bake in a 350-degree oven for 15–20 minutes. *Makes about 5 dozen.*

Once your husband's interest is rekindled you may find that you are forced to drag out some of your old hamburger recipes once in a while in self-defense. Turn up the lights, forgo the wine and quench the fire. After all, you can't very well get anything done while trying to dodge around him as he prostrates himself at your feet in blissful adoration.

Of savages and kings

3.

OF SAVAGES
AND
KINGS

Even if your soul mate has crinkly eyes and wears Irish fishermen's sweaters, he undoubtedly has a herd of bizarre friends from his past. They all do. The unfortunate thing is that we women never seem to hear about these friends until the vows have been said and the knot tied forever. Something in a man's deep subconscious must warn him to keep them under wraps, for usually the first we see of them is when they all appear at the wedding reception, resplendent in dark suits, loafers and white athletic socks.

But if you didn't know about them then, we'll just bet you do now. You can almost bank on the fact that one day he'll bring around a heterogeneous crowd of losers the likes of which are enough to make you fear for the future of the race. It isn't that all our men were creepy in their youth; it's just that they're genuinely nicer than the fairer sex and they'd never let an old buddy down.

Thus it is when Old Booper (they really did call each other things like that—we've even got an old college friend called Turtle, and another loving mother's Reyburn has been immortalized as Rabies) comes rambling into town, friend husband will graciously offer bed and board—without tips. He'll get a bemused look in his eye and ask if you ". . . remember Old Booper, honey? He played tight end the year Coach had me at QB against Branowski in the All-City game. Great year, that year. Yep. Old Booper . . ."

He'll neglect to mention that that was fifteen years ago in Junior High and they haven't seen or thought of each other since.

Then there's Ed Snate, the omnipresent fraternity brother. There are millions of them around. The way old fraternity brothers keep popping up, we're sure they must have been rammed in those houses like cross-pack sardines. And your man may have been on martinis for years, but when old Ed rolls in, watch him revert to beer. They'll trade stories and guffaw and you'll even hear them pitching beer cans at the fireplace before the evening's over. What's stranger, they'll belt each other in the arm (a mysterious male friendship rite that even Margaret Mead has yet to comprehend), pound each other's backs and slap thighs until you'll be sure it's some sort of masochistic karate parlor they're running. But would you just look at the fun they're having?

There's another group of men that belongs to your husband's covert life and they're rather discreetly referred to as business associates. First comes the pudgy tool and die entrepreneur from Terre Haute. He's given to creaky red-brown cordovans and simply wouldn't be without his lodge button. A genuine George Babbitt. Yessiree. Calls his wife the Missus and hauls out snaps of the kiddies at last year's Kiwanis picnic before you've even got the ice bucket in operation. Him you just endure.

And of course at the top of the heap is the Boss, most likely a florid-faced cardiac patient who tells shady stories and pats your knee a lot. Entertaining him is its own brand of nameless terror.

When you come right down to it, entertaining any of this species is a shattering experience. But it's really not cataclysmic, for these breeds usually live far enough away that 1) you don't see them too often, and 2) when they do jet into town it's without their wives. Anybody knows it's duck soup to entertain a man without his woman. They're pretty grateful for anything after hotel dining room fare and they won't even notice if you haven't had time to press the tablecloth and polish the snifters.

With either group, your tactics are about the same. The best idea is to leave the men pretty much alone—they're really not interested in your conversation right now. This doesn't mean you have to be the little brown wren of Maple Street, but just pleasantly unobtrusive before dinner. You can shine over the demitasse.

Food for either buddies or business cohorts should be something pretty wonderful. Of course Babbitt and the Boss rate the definite kingly treatment, for unfortunately you can't just hand them a 6-pack and give them a push in the direction of the den. So hold sway out of sight and work on some Lucullan magic. As is often the case with these relics of the past or the business world, you usually have only a few hours' notice of the impending crisis, but that's still enough time to be fairly languid about the whole thing. Besides, you won't miss much fascinating cocktail conversation if you have to be doing last-minute cooking while they're talking.

When dinner is served, this is where the pampering begins. If you're looking relaxed and lovely, exuding a 50-dollar aura of Chanel and presiding over an aromatic Entrecôte, those men will be so pea-green with jealousy over your husband's good fortune in finding you that your man will grin like an old Chessy. From now on he'll be the reigning monarch in their eyes.

In the following pages we've tried to recall a few of the menus we've used on some of Jack's and Ken's cronies. The only problem we haven't solved is that if it's too good, pretty soon they start planning more and more jaunts with stops in your city. But that's the price of success.

Eleventh Hour Appetizers

Finding something for them to nibble on during cocktails is no small task when you're pressed for time. But you must have at least one of these lying around in a cupboard somewhere:

OY VEYS

1 jar smoked salmon (lox)
1 3-ounce package cream cheese, softened

Remove the pieces of salmon from the jar and pat dry. Lay out flat and spread to edges with softened cream cheese. Roll up and fasten with toothpicks. Chill 2–3 hours. When quite firm, slice ½ inch thick, pinwheel fashion. *Makes about 2 dozen.*

TEENY WEENIES

1 package refrigerator biscuits or onion crescent rolls
1 small jar cocktail sausages (not Vienna sausages)
Hot mustard

Cut each biscuit or crescent roll into small shapes that will just fit around 1 teeny weenie. Spread each piece of dough with a little hot mustard, put on a weenie and wrap it up, pinching edges together. You should be able to see a portion of sausage peeking from each end. Now retrieve the directions for baking the biscuits from the wastebasket and follow them. Serve with more hot mustard for dunking. *Serves 4.*

CALCUTTA CURRIED PEANUTS

1 can salted roasted peanuts
2 teaspoons curry powder or more

Spread peanuts out in a single layer on a cookie sheet. Sprinkle with curry powder and stir gently to coat nuts with curry. Slide into a 350-degree oven for 5–10 minutes. Better keep a good stakeout on these as they'll burn in just the time it takes to fish the martini olives out of the jar. *Serves 4.*

PORKERS

1 dozen saltine crackers
1 dozen strips lean bacon, sliced thin

Wrap crackers in bacon strips neatly and broil, turning once, until bacon is crisp. That's all. *Serves 4.*

LOX AND CUCUMBERS

10 slices cucumber
10 thin slices lox

Lemon wedges
Cracked black pepper

Arrange cucumber slices on serving plate, top each with a slice of lox. Serve with lemon wedges and cracked black pepper. *Serves 2.*

We're usually four-square against dips, but this one really merits a landslide vote. The method of preparation seems kind of weird, but we suspect that's the secret to

DIANE'S DARK-HORSE DIP

2 jars Old English cheese
2 jars garlic cheese
4 scallions, tops and bottoms, chopped
1 clove garlic, crushed

¼ green pepper, minced
1 7-ounce can minced clams and ½ of the juice
Dash Worcestershire

Combine all ingredients and bake at 325 degrees for 40 minutes. Let stand for about 10 minutes before serving. *Makes 2½–3 cups.*

SARAH MARSHALL'S CHOPPED LIVER

¼ cup chicken fat
3 medium white onions, chopped

½ pound chicken livers
Salt and pepper
2 hard-cooked eggs, chopped

Push the chicken fat around in the skillet until fully rendered. Remove gristle and sauté onions until golden. Add chicken livers and cook slowly for 5 minutes or until done. Season to taste with salt and pepper. Combine with eggs and run it through a meat grinder or your blender. Chill. Serve with matzo wafers. *Makes 2 cups.*

This first menu is strictly for the savage variety, so save it for Booper's next visit. The dessert, though, has enough opulence for the president of AT&T . . .

BROILED PORTERHOUSE STEAK
BLEU CHEESE BUTTER   SPINACH-STUFFED TOMATOES
SAVORY BREAD
BABA BLACK SHEEP

PINOT NOIR

BLEU CHEESE BUTTER

½ stick softened butter   *1 tablespoon mustard*
Dash garlic powder   *¼ pound bleu cheese*

Blend butter and seasonings together. Sieve the bleu cheese and add to the butter mixture. Blend until creamy. Spoon onto hot steaks—a couple of tablespoons each will do wonderful and mysterious things to that plain beef. *Makes ¾ cup.*

SPINACH-STUFFED TOMATOES

1 10-ounce package frozen   *4 tomatoes, hollowed out and*
chopped spinach, cooked   *drained*
and drained   *4 mushroom caps, sautéed in*
Salt and pepper to taste   *butter*
Parmesan cheese

Season spinach with salt and pepper and a handful of Parmesan cheese. Stuff tomatoes with spinach mixture and top with a mushroom cap. Dot with butter. (*) Bake at 350 degrees for 15 minutes. *Serves 4.*

SAVORY BREAD

1 stick butter
¼ cup chopped parsley
¼ cup chopped green onion
2 tablespoons chopped celery
  leaves

Pinch each thyme and
  marjoram
French bread
Garlic salt

Melt butter, add parsley, green onion, celery leaves, thyme and marjoram. Muddle around for 5 or 10 minutes, then smear on slices of French bread. Sprinkle each slice with garlic salt, fit them back together in loaf shape and wrap in foil. (*) Heat at 400 degrees for 15 minutes. *Allow 3 slices per person.*

This is really only a shirt tail relation to Baba au Rhum, but delectable *and* undetectable:

BABA BLACK SHEEP

1 8-inch orange chiffon cake
  from the grocer
½ cup sugar

¾ cup apricot nectar
½ cup rum
1 teaspoon lemon juice

GLAZE:

3 tablespoons sugar
1 tablespoon cornstarch or
  more
½ cup apricot nectar

1 tablespoon light rum
Dash lemon juice
Candied cherries

Toast the cake in a 325-degree oven for 5 minutes. Cool. Place on intended serving plate and prick all over with a toothpick. Combine sugar, apricot nectar, rum and lemon juice. Bring just to a boil and cook for 5 minutes. Cool and ladle over cake. Allow to absorb and repeat until all sauce is absorbed. (You can rescue any sauce that collects in the center well with your turkey baster.) Chill 5–6 hours. Combine *Glaze* ingredients and cook 5–7 minutes or until thick and glossy. Cool slightly. Spread gently over the baba and chill 2–3 hours. Just before serving garnish with bits of candied cherries in 3–4 strategic spots. *Serves 10.*

Here's the Ed Snate Blue Plate Special; you're bound to have most of the ingredients right there on hand when the doorbell rings.

PIPERADE PIE

WATERCRESS SALAD   LEMON-OIL DRESSING

IT'S THE BERRIES

GREY RIESLING

PIPERADE PIE

1 9-inch pastry shell　　　*Healthy dash pepper*
Salad oil　　　　　　　　*1 cup cream*
1 cup green pepper strips　*3 medium eggs, beaten*
½ medium onion, sliced　　*4 ounces or more sharp*
2 tomatoes, sliced　　　　　*Cheddar cheese, grated*
1 teaspoon salt

Refrigerate pastry shell while you're concocting the Piperade. Heat oil in skillet and sauté green pepper and onion until soft. Add tomatoes and seasonings and cook for 2 or 3 minutes. Drain and save liquid. Add cream and reserved liquid to beaten eggs. Sprinkle half of grated cheese on bottom of pie shell. Spoon on vegetable mixture; then remaining cheese. Pour liquid gently over all. Bake at 375 degrees for 45 minutes or until knife comes clean out of the center. Let stand for 10 minutes before serving. *Serves 4.*

WATERCRESS SALAD

2 bunches watercress　　　*1 tablespoon capers*
1 head butter lettuce　　　*Lemon-Oil Dressing*

Wash and dry greens; tear in bite-sized pieces. Sprinkle with capers and toss with Lemon-Oil Dressing (see Index). *Serves 4.*

IT'S THE BERRIES

1 10-ounce package frozen raspberries
1 cup currant jelly
Tart raspberry sherbet

Heat frozen berries and jelly just to boiling point. Sieve and chill 3–4 hours. Serve over dishes of sherbet. *Makes 2½ cups sauce.*

This menu for an old army buddy may take him back to chow-line days, but he's bound to think the mess sergeant has improved since then.

ESTOFADO
BEER RICE   ICEBERG SALAD
WINE-SOUR CREAM DRESSING
ICED FRUIT COMPOTE   POLVORONES
BEER

ESTOFADO

1½ pounds boneless chuck,
cut for stew
1 onion, chopped
2 tablespoons oil
⅛ teaspoon garlic powder
4 tablespoons olive oil
½ cup tomato sauce

3 tablespoons vinegar
1 cup Burgundy wine
1 bay leaf
1 teaspoon oregano
Salt and pepper to taste
1 7-ounce can green chili
salsa

Brown meat and onion in oil in a Dutch oven, add remaining ingredients, cover and bring to boil. Reduce heat and simmer for 2 or 3 hours or until meat is tender. *Serves 4.*

BEER RICE

2 tablespoons olive oil
1 cup rice, uncooked

1 can onion soup
10 ounces beer

Heat oil in skillet, stir in rice and brown. Add liquids. Cover and simmer 25–30 minutes or until all liquid is absorbed. *Serves 6.*

WINE-SOUR CREAM DRESSING

1 cup sour cream
⅓ cup garlic wine vinegar
¼ teaspoon garlic powder

Stir all ingredients together. Serve tossed with torn iceberg lettuce. *Makes 1½ cups.*

ICED FRUIT COMPOTE

1 package frozen sliced
   peaches
1 package frozen raspberries

1 package frozen pineapple
   chunks
1 package frozen strawberries
Cointreau

Combine still frozen packages of fruit in large bowl and allow to thaw partially. Lace heavily with Cointreau to taste. Continue thawing until just a few ice crystals remain. Serve icy cold. *Serves 6–8.*

MEXICAN WEDDING CAKES
(*Polvorones*)

2 sticks butter, softened
½ cup powdered sugar
2½ cups flour

Dash salt
1 teaspoon vanilla
Powdered sugar

Mix butter, sugar, flour, salt and vanilla until smooth. Chill 1 hour. Form into walnut-sized balls and bake on cookie sheet at

375 degrees until light brown—about 15 minutes. Remove from cookie sheet and roll immediately in more powdered sugar. *Makes 4 dozen.*

———

Terre Haute doesn't really deserve anything as good as this next feast, but since you must endure the evening, you might as well have some reason for rejoicing. This is it.

FONDUE BOURGUIGNONNE

MOCK BÉARNAISE SAUCE ANCHOVY SAUCE

GARLIC SAUCE CURRY SAUCE

SWEET-SOUR SAUCE MUSTARD SAUCE

PLAIN FRENCH BREAD MUSHROOM SALAD

CHESS PIE

BURGUNDY

FONDUE BOURGUIGNONNE

1½ pounds tenderloin of beef
Peanut oil

Cube tenderloin into bite-sized pieces and set aside. Heat peanut oil in chafing dish or fondue dish. Each guest spears a chunk of tender beef and cooks his own meat in the hot oil. Makes for rather slow going sometimes, but no one seems to mind when the end result is this spectacular. Serve with a bevy of sauces. *Serves 3-4.*

MOCK BÉARNAISE SAUCE

1 teaspoon tarragon *3 shallots*
1 tablespoon tarragon vinegar *Pinch dry mustard*
1 cup mayonnaise

Soak tarragon in tarragon vinegar. Add mayonnaise, shallots and mustard. Into the blender with it for 1 minute. *Makes 1 cup.*

ANCHOVY SAUCE

2 teaspoons anchovy paste
1 cup mayonnaise

Combine thoroughly. *Makes 1 cup.*

GARLIC SAUCE

1 stick softened butter
1 clove garlic, minced

Cream together until smooth. *Makes ½ cup.*

CURRY SAUCE

2 teaspoons or more curry   Dash lemon juice
*   powder   1 10-ounce can beef gravy*
Dash garlic powder

Combine and taste for seasonings. *Makes 1½ cups.*

SWEET-SOUR SAUCE

Chung King makes a very good sweet-sour sauce. Try it.

MUSTARD SAUCE

If you can't get Spice Island's marvelous Champagne Mustard
sauce, try this:

1 cup mayonnaise   2 teaspoons tarragon vinegar
2 tablespoons sour cream   Salt
1½ tablespoons dry mustard

Combine mayonnaise, sour cream, mustard and vinegar and
muddle around. Salt to taste. *Makes 1 cup.*

MUSHROOM SALAD

DRESSING:

4 tablespoons lemon juice
4 tablespoons olive oil
2 tablespoons wine vinegar
1 tablespoon chives, chopped
1 teaspoon Dijon mustard

Fat pinches each of tarragon,
chervil
Salt and pepper to taste
1 tablespoon fresh parsley,
chopped

1 dozen medium mushrooms, Romaine or escarole
sliced

Combine dressing ingredients, shake and chill. Slice raw mushrooms and arrange on romaine or escarole leaves. Pour dressing over mushrooms. *Serves 4–6.*

CHESS PIE

One bite of this Southern favorite will have Terre Haute whistling "Dixie" . . .

1 stick butter, softened
1½ cups sugar
4 eggs, beaten well
¼ teaspoon salt
6 tablespoons cream

1 tablespoon vanilla
1 cup raisins
1 cup chopped walnuts
1 9-inch pastry shell
Sour cream

Cream butter and sugar together. Add remaining ingredients, beating after each addition. Pour into pastry shell. Bake at 450 degrees for 10 minutes, then reduce heat to 350 and bake until set, about 30 minutes. (Pie will still be slightly shaky in the center until cool.) Serve warm with globs of chilled sour cream. *Serves 6.*

When the Boss looms into view, get thee to a fish market . . .

FILET OF SOLE AMANDINE
SESAME TOASTS   BROILED ROQUEFORT TOMATOES
FLAMING HOT WINTER FRUIT
or
LECHEE NUTS HOROWITZ
DRY SAUTERNE

FILET OF SOLE AMANDINE

4 tablespoons butter   *Seasoned flour*
⅓ cup sliced natural almonds   Lemon wedges
1½ pounds filet of sole

Melt butter in skillet, sauté almonds in butter until golden.
Remove and reserve. Roll fish filets in seasoned flour and sauté
until done. Fish will flake easily when ready to serve. Remove
filets to platter and pour browned almonds over. Garnish with
lemon wedges. *Serves 3.*

SESAME TOASTS

3 slices firm bread, crusts removed
Butter
1 tablespoon sesame seeds

Cut each slice of bread into 3 sections. Spread with butter and
sprinkle with sesame seeds. Broil until golden and crisp. *Serves 3.*

BROILED ROQUEFORT TOMATOES

3 tablespoons Roquefort   *3 tomatoes, halved*
  cheese   *⅓ cup dry bread crumbs*
1 teaspoon Worcestershire   *Butter*
3 tablespoons cream cheese   *Paprika*
½ teaspoon onion powder

Mix together cheeses and seasonings. Blend well and smear on cut sides of tomatoes. Sprinkle with bread crumbs, dot with a little butter and dust with paprika. (*) Broil 10 minutes. *Serves 3–6.*

FLAMING HOT WINTER FRUIT

1 cup canned apricot halves
1 cup pitted dark sweet
    cherries
¾ cup canned pineapple
    chunks
¾ cup canned pear halves

A little of the juice of all four
    fruits
¼ teaspoon powdered cloves
¼ teaspoon cinnamon
1 tablespoon brown sugar
¼ cup white rum
3 tablespoons white rum

Hide those cans so you won't be discovered. Then pitch everything but the 3 tablespoons rum into a saucepan and simmer for 15 minutes. Transfer fruit mixture into a silver bowl. Heat the remaining rum (just barely—you don't want to burn off the alcohol) and pour over the fruit. Don't stir! Hold a match over the fruit immediately and if the gods are with you this evening, it'll flame beautifully. Prance to the table and serve in sherbet dishes. *Serves 4.*

When we took a promotion tour for *Saucepans and the Single Girl,* we hailed New York's most loquacious cabbie, who immediately plunged into his 20 questions. (It has long since been proven that all cabbies are either surly mutes or incurable motormouths.) When he discovered we'd written a cookbook, he waxed ecstatic. A lover of good cuisine, his specialty was Chinese food and he was Manhattan's Mogul of Tofu. Once rapport had been established, he insisted we call him Lechee Nut, for all his friends did. Lechee Nut Horowitz. We kid you not. So, Lechee Nut Horowitz, wherever you are, this one's for you . . .

LECHEE NUTS HOROWITZ

1 1-pound can lechee nuts in syrup
3 tablespoons green crème de menthe

Combine the lechee nuts and crème de menthe and chill several hours until icy cold. Spoon 4–5 lechee nuts into each sherbet dish and ladle a little of the syrup over each serving. *Serves 4.*

This next menu is exciting enough for the Chairman of the Board, but with a built-in safety feature. You can be assured that somewhere in that Paella, there's something that even the most picky eater would enjoy. If not, you can always hand him his hat and coat.

POMPOUS PAELLA

GARLIC BREAD   TOSSED SALAD—AVOCADO DRESSING

FLAN

MOSELLE

POMPOUS PAELLA

3 whole chicken breasts, cut in half
Salt and pepper
½ teaspoon garlic powder
4 tablespoons olive oil
1 onion, chopped
2 cups diced ham
2 7-ounce cans clams, drained
1 dozen large shrimp, cleaned and deveined
3 lobster tails, cut in thirds, shell intact
1 tomato, cut in eighths
1 10-ounce package frozen peas
1 10-ounce package frozen artichoke hearts
2 13-ounce cans chicken broth
⅛ teaspoon saffron
2 cups regular rice
2 medium pimientos, cut in strips
6 whole clams, scrubbed

Wipe chicken breasts dry. Sprinkle with salt and pepper and garlic powder. Brown in your largest skillet (about 16 inches) in olive oil. Add chopped onion and sauté until soft. Add ham, clams, shrimp, lobster, tomato, peas and artichoke hearts; stir and simmer for 5 minutes. Add broth and saffron and simmer, covered for 10 minutes. Add rice and pimientos, stir again and simmer 15 more minutes. Push in clams, cover and simmer 10–15 more minutes or until clams open and rice has absorbed all of the moisture. The nice thing is that if they're discussing stock options or vice-presidencies you can quite successfully stick it in a 250-degree oven for an indeterminate amount of time. *Serves 6.*

AVOCADO DRESSING

2 avocados
2 tablespoons lemon juice
½ cup sour cream
½ teaspoon onion powder

¾ teaspoon salt
½ teaspoon horseradish
¼ teaspoon Worcestershire

Peel and pit avocados; puree in blender. Add remaining ingredients and mix thoroughly. Makes 2 cups. Serve over tossed mixed greens.

Leave it to the Latins to dream up a lazy man's crème brûlée. The French may have originated it, but this is so simple yet so good, that even General de Gaulle couldn't look down his nose at it.

FLAN

1 cup sugar
4 eggs, beaten
1 pint can sweetened
  condensed milk

1 cup water
1 teaspoon vanilla
¼ cup brandy

Place sugar in bottom of deep glass pan and place over burner. Stir constantly over medium heat until sugar melts and turns a lovely caramel color. Jiggle the pan around until caramel coats the whole thing; set aside to cool. In another bowl, mix eggs, milk, water and vanilla. Pour over cooled caramel. Cover pan and place in a larger pan. Put about 2 cups water in the bottom of the larger pan. Now put the whole apparatus in the oven at 350 degrees for an hour or so or until a knife inserted in the center comes out clean and shiny. Chill 3–4 hours. Turn out onto serving plate, caramel side up. Pour heated brandy over the Flan and ignite. Serve flaming. *Serves 6.*

Coddling the poor dear

4.

CODDLING THE POOR DEAR

A man does need coddling. He needs it when he loses a client and his ego is as flat as a day-old balloon. He needs it when he has a cold—although, as you know, men never have colds. One sneeze and they are in the Valley of the Shadow of Death. He needs it when the car won't start, even though he has always claimed he once drove at Le Mans. He'll need even more coddling when the serviceman arrives and patiently explains that the car is out of gas.

There are many ways to coddle a man, many ways to make him feel that even Prince Rainier with his kingdom, Grace Kelly *and* his own casino is a pauper by comparison. When your husband has a bad case of the mean reds a simple thing like finding he actually has a clean shirt in the morning can make him see the sunshine of your smile. Or perhaps just discovering a frosty glass nesting in the freezer awaiting his evening cocktail will make him bless the day he found you. Of course sometimes things are so bad that nothing short of looking in the mirror and discovering that he's suddenly become Cary Grant will perk him up. If this is the case all you can do is tighten your apron sash and prepare for the rough days ahead.

For the most part this chapter deals less with this type of catastrophic situation than with day to day coddling. This is what endears you to him in the long run anyway. In this chapter you will find recipes for man-sized snacks, weekend lunches, diet dinners and for gourmet lunches to take to the office. Who knows, if you coddle him enough he might decide to coddle you right back. And did breakfast in bed really ever hurt anyone?

The only way to keep a determined snacker from undermining the plans you've made for that leftover prime rib so carefully hidden behind the cantaloupe is for you to head him off at the pantry with something equally interesting. The easiest ambush is popcorn. In addition, some men think popping corn over glowing embers is very romantic and who are we to complain?

Buttering Him Up

Noshes to keep him happy while he's watching the Packers score a field goal or perusing a heady issue of *Playboy*:

1. Chop the contents of a jar of dried beef and dump into a frying pan with ¼ cup butter. Pour the beef and butter over 8 cups of popcorn and serve immediately. (No salt or you'll spend the night at the water jug.)

2. Stir 1 tablespoon lemon juice into ¼ cup melted butter. Pour over 8 cups popped corn and toss.

3. Melt ¼ cup butter with 1 tablespoon sesame seeds over medium heat in a small frying pan. Shake the pan often as you heat it. Continue heating and shaking to the beat of a fast frug until the butter froths and turns golden. Pour over 8 cups of popped corn and toss.

4. Sprinkle 2 tablespoons of fresh dill or 2 teaspoons of dried dill over already buttered hot popcorn.

5. Stir 1 teaspoon curry powder into ¼ cup melted butter. Pour over 8 cups of popped corn and toss.

6. Toss 2 tablespoons of grated Parmesan cheese with already buttered popcorn.

7. If you don't feel like going to even these meager extremes just toss the popcorn with seasoned salt. It makes a difference.

If your husband finally reaches the point where he would rather gnaw on a chair leg than face another piece of popcorn, you might go to a bit more trouble to trot out these snacks.

TIJUANA TREATS

1 package piecrust mix   *½ teaspoon Tabasco*
1 cup finely grated sharp   *Paprika*
    Cheddar cheese

Mix the piecrust mix with the cheese until the Cheddar is evenly distributed. Add the Tabasco to the water called for on the package directions. Stir in the liquid with a fork. Form the dough into a ball (*) and roll out. Cut into squares and sprinkle with paprika. Bake on an ungreased baking sheet in a 375 degree oven for 5–8 minutes. Serve immediately or reheat for later snacking.

THE MOST TOAST

1 cup grated Cheddar cheese   *Paprika*
2 tablespoons mayonnaise   *Worcestershire*
2 teaspoons cream   *Garlic powder*
1 teaspoon finely chopped   *4 slices white toast*
    onion   *2 slices bacon, partially*
½ teaspoon dry mustard   *cooked*

Combine all of the ingredients except the toast and bacon. Blend until smooth. (*) Remove crusts from the toast, spread the toast with cheese mixture and cut each slice into 6 strips. Top each with a small piece of bacon. Bake in a very hot oven (450 degrees) for 5 or 6 minutes. This is really quite a bit of trouble so we suggest reserving it for those nights when he has brought you a square-cut emerald from Tiffany's or a dozen long-stemmed yellow roses.

PEANUTS IN QUILTS
(Distantly related to Pigs in Blankets)

1 can refrigerator biscuits	*4 slices crisp bacon*
½ cup peanuts	*Mayonnaise*

Split and fill unbaked biscuits with a little pile of peanuts, a bit of crisp crumbled bacon and a dab of mayonnaise. This is rather by guess and by golly, but you can't go too wrong on the proportions if you are light on the mayonnaise. Bake according to directions on the package of biscuits. *Makes 12 biscuits.*

Saturdays' Heroes

Weekend lunches rank just below oven-cleaning and scrubbing the bathtub on any woman's list of favorite events. So when the man in your life comes loping in with grass in his cuffs and hunger in his eyes, maybe these ideas will help you over the hump. An aspirin wouldn't hurt either.

MAINE LINE ROLLS

2 teaspoons prepared mustard	*½ cup mayonnaise*
1 teaspoon chopped parsley	*¾ pound fresh lobster (or 2 cans—5 ounces each)*
1 teaspoon chopped chives	*2 tablespoons lemon juice*
¼ teaspoon cayenne pepper	*½ cup diced celery*
¼ cup chopped onion	*6 English muffins, split and toasted*
½ teaspoon salt	

Mix the mustard, parsley, chives, pepper, onion and salt with the mayonnaise. When you have put the tops back on those bottles, wipe your brow and drain, shell and dice the lobster. Now mix the lobster, lemon juice and celery in a bowl and stir in the mayonnaise mixture. Divide the mixture evenly and spread on the muffins. Place the tops on the muffins. *Serves 6.*

WILD WILD WESTWICHES

2 eggs
¼ cup milk
½ cup chopped onions
¼ cup chopped green pepper
½ cup finely chopped ham

¼ teaspoon salt
Dash pepper
4 French rolls, split
1 tablespoon butter

Beat the eggs until fluffy, stir in the milk, onion, green pepper, ham and salt and pepper. Meanwhile toast the split French rolls in the broiler. Melt butter in a skillet and pour in two oblongs of the egg mixture. This can be rather tricky, so use a ½-cup measure to judge the amount and pour carefully. Cook over a low heat until firm. Turn and cook the other side for about a minute. Repeat the same process with the remaining egg mixture. Slip the egg blob into the split rolls. You can keep the rolls you have already made warm in a 225 degree oven while you are dealing with the rest. *Serves 4.*

IRISH REBELLION SANDWICH

2 cups shredded cabbage
⅓ cup mayonnaise
1 tablespoon chili sauce
1 teaspoon minced onion
¼ teaspoon salt
4 hamburger buns, split and
    lightly toasted

1 4-ounce package sliced
    corned beef or four slices
    leftover corned beef
Prepared mustard
Dry mustard

Mix the shredded cabbage with the mayonnaise, chili sauce, onion and salt. Spoon mixture onto the bottom half of the buns.

Line up the slices of corned beef on top of the cabbage. Spread the top of the bun with prepared mustard to which you have added a dash of dry mustard for extra zing. *Serves 4 ruddy rebels.*

NO WORRY CURRY SANDWICHES

The curry blends so well with the eggs that even the most dedicated anti-curry man will come sneaking back for more.

6 *hard-cooked eggs, chopped*
½ *cup mayonnaise*
1 *teaspoon curry, or more to taste*
½ *cup chopped stuffed or ripe olives*
½ *teaspoon salt*
¼ *teaspoon pepper*
8 *slices cracked wheat bread, buttered*
Lettuce

Mix all of the ingredients (except the bread and lettuce of course). Spread the curried egg mixture between the bread slices. Place a handsome green lettuce leaf on top of the sandwich just before closing it up. *Serves 4.*

DOWN EASTERN SANDWICH

1 *can oysters (10 ounce)*
Flour
1 *egg*
1 *teaspoon water*
Cracker meal
2 *tablespoons butter*
4 *toasted, buttered buns*
Dill pickle slices
½ *cup chili sauce*
4 *teaspoons prepared horseradish*
Lime wedges
Tomatoes, sliced

Sprinkle the oysters with flour and let stand for about 15 minutes. Beat the egg with water and dip the oysters in the mixture. Roll in cracker meal and allow to rest for another 15 minutes. Sizzle in butter until a good toasty brown. Arrange oysters on buns and top with dill pickle slices. Whip up a sauce of the chili and horseradish and plaster on the buns before closing. Serve with lime wedges and sliced tomatoes. *Serves 4.*

STEAK AND SALAMI HEROES

½ cup soft butter
1 tablespoon chopped chives
1 tablespoon prepared
* mustard*
½ teaspoon Worcestershire
6 French rolls

2 club steaks about an inch
* thick*
Salt and pepper
½ pound Italian salami,
* thinly sliced*
Parsley

Mix the butter, chives, mustard and Worcestershire to form a soft spread. Smear on both halves of sliced French rolls. Trim excess fat from the steaks and broil until medium rare (about 4 minutes on each side) or however you prefer them. Salt and pepper to taste. Slice steaks thinly on the bias. Pile the steak and salami on the buttered rolls and serve garnished with parsley. *Serves 6.*

LYNDON'S LEFTOVERS

How're you going to keep him down on the ranch after he's seen D.C.?

4 French rolls
2 cups canned red kidney
* beans, drained*
3 tablespoons kidney-bean
* liquid*
1¼ teaspoons salt
¾ teaspoon chili powder
¼ teaspoon ground black
* pepper*

⅛ teaspoon garlic powder
½ cup shredded lettuce
¼ pound sliced cooked turkey
* or ham*
1 avocado in thin slices
1 large green pepper, cut in
* rings ⅛ inch thick*

Cut the rolls in half and tear out their soft centers. Combine the kidney beans, liquid, salt, chili powder, pepper and garlic. Heat them in a saucepan and put through a sieve or in the blender to form a paste. Cool. Spread over the bottom halves of the rolls. Cover with shredded lettuce. Top with the meat, avocado and green pepper. Cover with the remaining half of the rolls. *Serves 4.*

Brown-Bagging It

If your husband works in an office, whether he is the purveyor of paper clips or president of the corporation, he may well have fallen into the loathsome habit of ordering a chopped egg on white and a waxy carton of milk for lunch. Of course there are long martini-prefaced business lunches occasionally, but he can't indulge in those too often if he hopes to keep two steps ahead of your Saks bill. So when he's stuck behind his desk for the midday repast why not suggest that he bring lunch from home? If he's embarrassed to brown-bag it in front of his buddies, and refuses to carry a Mickey Mouse lunch pail he can always pack a few goodies in his attaché case. Of course now you must come up with something better than the drugstore, so here are a few suggestions to start your culinary imagination functioning.

To Wet His Whistle

(Which hopefully is not being used as commentary on his secretary's legs.)

ICY BLACK BEAN SOUP

½ cup canned chicken broth   ½ small onion
¼ cup sherry   ¾ cup milk
1 10½-ounce can black bean
   soup

Toss the broth, sherry, soup and onion in your blender. Mix at high speed for a couple of minutes. Add milk and blend until smooth. Refrigerate. When it is thoroughly chilled place in a cold thermos bottle. Include a well-wrapped scallion to be used as a swizzle stick. *Serves 3.*

CURRY SOUP

1 can cream of chicken soup *1 tablespoon butter*
½ can water *Snipped chives*
1½–2½ teaspoons curry *Thin slices of apple*
½ can milk

Combine the soup, water, curry, milk and butter in a saucepan and heat until bubbly. Toss in some snipped chives and pour into a thermos that has been warmed with hot water. Include some apple slices in a plastic bag for him to float on top of the soup. *Serves 3.*

VICHYSSOISE

1 can frozen potato soup *2 tablespoons dry sauterne*
1 soup can half and half *Snipped chives*

Defrost soup and place in a blender with the half and half. Add sauterne and blend at a medium speed for about 2 minutes. Add snipped chives and pour into a chilled thermos. *Serves 4.*

MARTINIS

If he insists that lunch is not lunch without a wee snort, you might mix a *small* batch of his favorite formula martini (don't fill the thermos unless you want him to be a menace to navigation all afternoon). We wouldn't presume to print a recipe for a martini as our husbands think ours taste like motor oil, so you'd best ask him or consult a reliable bartending guide.

FRESH LEMONADE

A thermos of this will have him reminiscing all afternoon about boyhood summers on the farm, and his air-conditioned office will be filled with the fragrance of new-mown hay.

3 lemons
1 cup sugar
3 cups water

Slice lemons thin and place rind and all in the bottom of a bowl. Pour on sugar and pound with a vengeance. Add water and chill. Strain into a frosty thermos. *Serves 6.*

Sangría (see Index) would also be a good addition to a lunch a-go-go.

The Meat of the Matter

Most men, in their heart of hearts, really love sandwiches. But they love good hearty sandwiches, not tiny cucumber and crabmeat dainties. So give him what he likes—good chunks of meat between firm slices of bread.

The bread should be from your favorite bakery or, better yet, home-baked. Do we sense a shiver of disbelief? Well, stay with us. What we mean by home-baked are those convenient frozen loaves of dough you can buy at the supermarket and defrost while you are weeding the marigolds or checking your dark roots. Of course you can just dump the loaf in the oven as is and still be the heroine of the piece, but if your ego feels the need of a really good shoring up try this: Before you put the defrosted bread in the pan ooze it out on your breadboard and sprinkle it with whatever comes into view such as dill weed, basil, summer savory, cheese, onion soup mix or sugar and cinnamon. Turn it over to a clean side and keep this up until the bread seems well saturated and then form back into a loaf, let rise and bake as usual. We guarantee that you will be the queen of the hop in your house.

As for the fillings of the sandwiches, try different combinations with hefty slices of meat from the deli. For instance try roast beef with lemon mayonnaise (mayonnaise mixed with lemon juice and chopped chives); roast lamb with curry mayonnaise (simply season the mayonnaise with curry to taste) or ham with chutney. And though we hesitate to mention it, don't forget peanut butter and jellies—most men never outgrow them.

In addition to sandwiches, try cold leftover Piperade (see Index) or . . .

GYPSY'S PASTIES

¼ cup sherry	*½ pound round steak, cubed*
1 small onion, finely chopped	*into ½-inch pieces*
2 tablespoons snipped parsley	*1 potato, peeled and cut into*
¾ teaspoon salt	*¼-inch cubes*
⅛ teaspoon pepper	*1 package piecrust mix*
1 teaspoon MSG	*1 egg*
⅛ teaspoon thyme	*1 tablespoon water*

Mix together the sherry, onion, parsley, salt, pepper, MSG and thyme. Marinate the steak and potato in this mixture for about 2 hours. Drain off the liquid. Prepare piecrust dough as your package label directs. Now grease a large cookie sheet and set your oven at 350 degrees. Roll out half of the dough and cut into 3 6-inch circles. Beat the egg with the water and brush edge of each circle with some of the egg mixture. Place ½ cup of the meat mixture in the center of each circle. Roll out the rest of the dough and cut out 3 more circles of the same size. Lay 1 over each meat-covered circle and press together to seal in the filling. (*) Brush with beaten egg. Bake for about 1 hour and 15 minutes or until golden and crisp. Cool and wrap in waxed paper. Refrigerate until ready to pack in his lunch. These can also be frozen for future use. *Serves 3.*

Gourmet Goodies

These are the items that separate the great lunch from the lackluster.

HAM ROLL-UPS

2 slices prosciutto ham, or   *Sharp mustard*
   other thinly sliced ham   *2 slices of his favorite cheese*

Spread the ham with the mustard. Place the cheese on top.
Roll up and fasten with 2 toothpicks. *Serves 2.*

COLD CHICKEN BOSOMS

Known in less genteel circles as chicken breasts.

Chicken bosoms (as many as you would like to prepare)
¼ cup butter or oil
Seasoned flour (with salt, pepper, paprika—you know the
   routine)

Pat the chicken bosoms dry with a paper towel. Melt the butter
or pour the oil into a flat pan with sides (a cake pan does nicely).
Coat the chicken with the seasoned flour and place in the pan.
Stash in a 350 degree oven for about an hour and 15 minutes,
turning once. Remove from the oven and chill.

SHRIMP WITH GREEN MAYONNAISE

¾ cup mayonnaise   *1 teaspoon chopped chives*
¼ cup finely chopped raw   *¼ teaspoon Dijon mustard*
   spinach   *½ pound shrimp—shelled,*
½ teaspoon tarragon   *deveined and cooked*
2 tablespoons chopped
   parsley

Combine all of the ingredients but the shrimp and blend well.
Refrigerate for 2 hours. Pack into a jar and place shrimp in a
plastic bag to stow in the lunch bag. The shrimp are to be dipped
into the mayonnaise when lunchtime hunger pangs strike.
Serves 2.

FANCY DEVILED EGGS

*3 eggs, hard-cooked and
  shelled*
2 tablespoons red caviar
*1 tablespoon grated onion (or
  1 teaspoon instant onion)*

Dash Tabasco (be gentle)
Chopped parsley
Mayonnaise if needed

Cut the eggs in half lengthwise and remove yolks. Put the yolks in a bowl and mash with the caviar and seasonings until they form a paste. Stuff the whites with the mixture and garnish with a bit of parsley. Chill. *Serves 2.*

VEGETABLES À LA GREQUE

Asparagus, artichoke hearts, green onions, leeks, tiny eggplants, zucchini, fresh mushrooms, celery hearts, fennel, cauliflower flowerets, tiny whole carrots or small white onions can all be marinated in this sauce and included in a lunch.

1½ cups water
¼ cup olive oil
Juice of 2 lemons
1 teaspoon salt
2–3 garlic cloves

1 bay leaf
Sprig of parsley
1 teaspoon thyme
½ teaspoon white pepper
Dash Tabasco

Combine all the ingredients in a saucepan and bring to a boil. Boil for 5 minutes and add whatever vegetable you have chosen. Simmer until just tender. Let the vegetable cool in the sauce, remove the garlic and chill. Pack in a covered jar. *Makes a scant 2 cups.*

Other good things to include are small cherry tomatoes with a shaker full of seasoned salt; marinated artichoke hearts, available in jars; and wedges of imported cheese with crackers and grapes.

For His Sweet Tooth

EXCLUSIVE CHOCOLATE CHEESECAKES

1 package no-bake
cheesecake
4 tablespoons sugar
⅓ cup butter or margarine,
melted

1½ cups cold milk
1 tablespoon sugar
1 ounce unsweetened
chocolate, melted

Mix the graham cracker crumbs from cheesecake mix with sugar and melted butter. Place a paper cupcake liner in 9 3-inch muffin pan cups. Spoon about 1 tablespoon of the crumb mixture into each paper liner. Press the mixture evenly on the bottom and sides of the liner. Refrigerate until firm. Pour the milk into a small bowl and add cheesecake filling from the package and 1 tablespoon sugar. Beat until well blended—about 3 minutes with an electric mixer. Add melted chocolate and beat 1 minute longer. Spoon some of the filling into each graham cracker shell. Refrigerate. *9 servings.*

COOKIES I

20 double size graham crackers
1 can sweetened condensed milk
1 package chocolate chips

Set oven at 350 degrees. Crumble graham crackers. Add milk and chocolate chips. Mix and smear into an 8-inch baking pan. Bake at 350 degrees until golden on top, about 30 minutes. Cool and cut into 16 squares.

COOKIES II

1½ cups flour
1 cup brown sugar
1 teaspoon salt
¾ cup soft butter

2 cups oatmeal
2 cups jelly, jam or preserves
¾ cup chopped pecans

Combine the flour, brown sugar and salt. Cut in butter until crumbly. Add oatmeal and stir. Place half of the mixture in the bottom of a 9×13 pan. Spread on the jam. Top with the remaining mixture and sprinkle on pecans. Bake in a 375 degree oven for 25 minutes. Cool and cut into 24 bars.

Skinny Food

If your husband has been complaining about the cleaner shrinking his clothes, or if you have noticed a certain creeping chubbiness coming on the scene, it is time to put him on a secret diet. By the way, this works equally well for you if you've been making a wide detour around the bathroom scale lately. The only real secret about these menus is that they're so good he'll never know what you're up to.

Unless he eats like good King Henry VIII at breakfast and lunch he should be able to lose a bit of himself with these dinners.

HUSKY MUSHROOMS

RICKSHAW CHICKEN

STEAMED RICE

FRESH BROCCOLI IN CHERVIL BUTTER

LEMON SOUFFLÉ

HUSKY MUSHROOMS

8 mushroom crowns	*Dash Tabasco*
½ carton skim milk cottage cheese	*Dash Worcestershire*
	½ teaspoon celery salt
1 tablespoon minced onions	*¼ teaspoon dry mustard*

Wash the mushrooms and hollow out the stem a bit. Mix the cheese, onions and spices and place a bit of the mixture in the hollows. Serve chilled. *Serves 2.*

RICKSHAW CHICKEN

¼ pound sliced fresh
   mushrooms
1 tablespoon vegetable oil
1 cup celery, sliced on a slant
¼ cup thinly sliced green
   onions
¼ cup sliced water chestnuts
¼ cup sliced green pepper
¼ cup sliced bamboo shoots

1½ cups chicken broth
1 tablespoon soy sauce
¼ teaspoon salt
1½ cups diced, cooked
   chicken
1½ tablespoons cornstarch
2 tablespoons water
1 teaspoon sugar
½ teaspoon powdered ginger

Sauté mushrooms in oil until limp and glossy. Add celery and green onions and cook for 3 minutes. Add water chestnuts, green pepper, bamboo shoots, chicken broth, soy sauce and salt. Simmer for 5 minutes and then add chicken. Dissolve cornstarch in cold water, add sugar and ginger to mixture and stir into chicken miscellany. Cook until the sauce thickens. *Serves 2 or 3.*

STEAMED RICE
(See Index)

FRESH BROCCOLI IN CHERVIL BUTTER

1 pound fresh broccoli
½ cup lightly salted water
1 tablespoon butter
1 teaspoon chervil

¼ teaspoon garlic powder
Salt and pepper
2 tablespoons lemon juice

Toss away all the large leaves and the tough part of the broccoli stalks. Wash what's left in several waters and drain. Halve each stalk lengthwise and cook in lightly salted water for 15 minutes or until crisp but tender. Melt the butter and stir in the chervil, garlic powder, salt and pepper and lemon juice. Roll the broccoli in the mixture and serve hot. *Serves 2.*

LEMON SOUFFLÉ

2 *egg yolks*	*Grated rind ½ lemon*
3 *tablespoons sugar*	3 *egg whites*
2 *tablespoons lemon juice*	*Dash salt*

Beat the yolks and 2 tablespoons of the sugar together. Add the lemon juice and rind. Beat the whites until they form soft peaks. Add the rest of the sugar and the salt to the whites and continue beating until they are sturdy and stiff, but not dry. Fold a bit of the whites into the yolk mixture and then carefully swish the yolk mixture through the rest of the whites. The resulting batter should be well mixed but as soft as a spring breeze. Pour into a small soufflé dish that has been buttered and sugared. Bake in a 400-degree oven for about 10–15 minutes. Serve at once. *Serves 2.*

SMOKED OYSTERS IN CHERRY TOMATOES

SLIM SOLE

CARRIED AWAY SPINACH

FRENCH STRAWBERRIES

SMOKED OYSTERS IN CHERRY TOMATOES

Hollow out the middle of the tiny tomatoes and fill each with a smoked oyster.

SLIM SOLE

1½ *teaspoons butter*	*Pepper*
1½ *teaspoons olive oil*	½ *cup seedless white grapes*
2 *slices onion*	¼ *cup dry white wine*
1 *pound filet of sole*	1 *teaspoon brandy*
¾ *teaspoon salt*	*Minced parsley*

Melt the butter and oil in a pan and add the onion slices. Sprinkle the fish with salt and pepper, then add to the pan. Cook slowly about 10 minutes and sprinkle with black pepper. Turn the fish and add the grapes. Continue to cook slowly for 3–5 minutes. Drain the fat from the pan and add the wine and brandy. Simmer gently for 10 minutes without allowing the liquid to boil. Pretty the fish up with a bit of minced parsley before serving. *Serves 2.*

CARRIED AWAY SPINACH

1 package frozen spinach   *1 tablespoon butter*
½ teaspoon caraway seeds   *1 teaspoon lemon juice*

Cook the spinach according to package directions, drain thoroughly. Crush the caraway seeds in a mortar (or use the back of a spoon in a wooden salad bowl). Work in the butter and lemon juice and toss with the hot spinach. *Serves 2.*

FRENCH STRAWBERRIES

½ pound strawberries
½ teaspoon artificial sweetener
½ cup red wine

Wash and hull the plump and rosy strawberries. Mix the sweetener with the wine and pour onto the fruit. Chill for at least an hour before serving. *Serves 2.*

BOGUS BORSCHT
LAMB TOUCHÉ
GREEN SALAD WITH BLEU CHEESE DRESSING
PEACH SHERBET

BOGUS BORSCHT

1 cup vegetable juice cocktail,   *Yogurt*
   chilled   *Dill weed*
1½ cups chilled buttermilk

Stir the juice and milk together and pour into soup bowls. Top with a dollop of yogurt and a sprinkle of dill weed. *Serves 2.*

LAMB TOUCHÉ

¾ pound lean lamb
1 lemon
Chopped parsley

Cut the lamb into 10–12 pieces and slice the lemon. Alternate a piece of meat with a slice of lemon on 2 skewers. Broil for 5 minutes. Sprinkle with chopped parsley and serve very hot. *Serves 2.*

GREEN SALAD WITH BLEU CHEESE DRESSING

DRESSING:

1 cup creamed cottage cheese   *2 tablespoons oil*
½ cup yogurt   *Salt and pepper*
4-ounce wedge bleu cheese

1 head romaine, washed,
  drained and torn

Combine all of the dressing ingredients in a blender and mix until smooth. Yields 2 cups of dressing. Use a portion of it on the romaine leaves and save the rest of the dressing for a later salad. *Serves 2.*

PEACH SHERBET

½ cup plain yogurt   *¼ cup honey*
1 cup sliced fresh peaches   *¼ cup orange juice*

Combine all of the ingredients in a blender and whirl for one minute. Pour into a refrigerator tray and freeze until firm around the edges. Turn into a chilled bowl and beat until smooth and fluffy. Return to the tray and freeze until set. Remove from the freezer about 15 minutes before serving. *Serves 2.*

GOLDEN VEAL ROLLS
MARTYR'S MUSHROOMS
HERBED SALAD BOWL
MOCHA POTS

GOLDEN VEAL ROLLS

2 hard-cooked eggs
2 veal scallops
Salt and pepper to taste
1 onion, sliced
¼ teaspoon thyme

1 bay leaf
2 cups tomato juice
½ teaspoon salt
¼ teaspoon pepper

Wrap each egg in a veal scallop that has been salted and peppered. Secure carefully with a string. Place the veal rolls in a small casserole. Add onions, thyme and bay leaf. Moisten with the tomato juice. Add more salt and pepper. (*) Cook in a 350-degree oven for about 1 hour. Before serving remove the string and cut each roll in half so that the egg yolk peeks out. *Serves 2.*

MARTYR'S MUSHROOMS

He'll lose that depressingly self-sacrificing air once he tastes these!

½ pound mushrooms
Water
Lemon juice
½ cup skim milk

1 teaspoon salt
½ teaspoon pepper
1 tablespoon parsley, chopped

Clean the mushrooms and soak them in water with a bit of lemon juice added. Heat the skim milk with salt and pepper. Slice the mushrooms, add to the milk and simmer over low heat. When they are cooked, drain off the milk. Serve sprinkled with chopped parsley. *Serves 2.*

HERBED SALAD BOWL

¼ *head iceberg lettuce, very*
  crisp and cold
¼ *head endive*
¼ *cup diced celery*
¼ *cup diced green pepper*
¼ *teaspoon salt*

¼ *teaspoon crumbled*
  oregano
Pinch *garlic powder*
1 *teaspoon lemon juice*
1 *tablespoon oil*
¼ *cup shredded carrots*

Tear the lettuce into bite-sized pieces. Toss into a salad bowl with the celery, green pepper, salt, oregano, garlic, lemon juice and oil. Toss lightly and then scatter shredded carrots over all before giving it a thorough tossing. *Serves 2.*

MOCHA POTS

1 *envelope low-calorie*
  chocolate pudding mix
¼ *cup evaporated skim milk*
⅔ *cup strong black coffee*

½ *ounce semi-sweet chocolate*
½ *teaspoon artificial*
  sweetener
¾ *teaspoon brandy extract*

Stir the pudding mix into the milk and coffee in a saucepan. Add the chocolate and sweetener and stir over a low heat until the chocolate is melted and the mixture has reached a bare simmer. Remove from the heat and add brandy extract. Pour into 2 individual molds and chill. *Serves 2.*

Now that you have seen how easy it is to coddle your way into the heart of your man, one last word of advice. Before you go to all of this trouble just be sure he's worth it. No good cook would coddle a bad egg.

The boys

5.

THE
BOYS

Like some ancient and irrefutable rite of spring, all men hear the annual call of the wild. The "wild" may be five-card stud or partridges in season; it really doesn't matter when they feel the need to get together for a little scratching and a lot of lying. Thus it is when hunting season sneaks in even the most impeccable male is compelled to sport a six-day growth and go scrounging through the Goodwill bag for his old red plaid shirt. And the man who can blandly fling down a ten-spot for the sake of a few paltry pieces of pasteboard and the approval of the Friday night poker club is the same turncoat who dogs around behind you all day mumbling and pointedly switching off lights.

When the moon is high and the wolves begin to howl, there's not much you can do about it, for at this time a man's logic fails him in much the same way yours does when a pair of silk crepe hostess pajamas that you really don't need is marked down a full five dollars. Just remember if those p.j.'s are food for your soul, a conclave with the backroom boys is equally good for his tortured ego. Bear with it and if the poker party is at your house, remember any good dirty jokes you might overhear.

So while they're all in there raising a smoke screen and deciding whether old Roberta Culpepper back in P.S. 67 Did or Didn't, you can confine yourself to the galley and sling together something hearty and filling to nourish the Nathan Detroit in each of them.

Men we've otherwise known and loved have offered a few.

words on men, food and poker parties, stag parties or whatever other kind of noisy ballyhoo it is you might be stuck with. It seems men have no inclination to stop this fraternization long enough to eat anything in any polite and tidy fashion, so it should be a morsel they can dip, dunk, munch, or just generally sprinkle over the immediate vicinity. Skip the Welsh Rarebit and serve up something simple along with a flagon of ale and then forget the whole business. Besides, that way you'll have time to sneak out with the other cast-off wives and catch the latest Paul Newman flick. On second thought, don't. You'll only feel worse.

FULL HOUSE SANDWICH

EACH SANDWICH REQUIRES:

2 slices bread, large loaf
   variety
¾ cup crabmeat
2 tablespoons mayonnaise
⅛ teaspoon salt

½ small avocado, sliced thin
Lemon juice
3 slices bacon, fried and
   drained

While the bread is toasting, mix the crabmeat with the mayonnaise and salt. Arrange avocado slices on 1 slice of toast, top with crab mixture and sprinkle with lemon juice. Arrange bacon slices on top and cover with a second slice of toast. *Serves 1.*

HAMBURGER BY THE YARD

2 pounds ground round
1 1-pound can Mexican-style
   whole kernel corn, drained
¾ cup chopped onion
2 eggs
2 tablespoons mustard

2 teaspoons salt
½ teaspoon seasoned pepper
1 loaf French bread, split in
   half lengthwise
¾ cup grated sharp Cheddar
   cheese

Set oven at 350 degrees. Combine all ingredients but the last 2. (*) Mound on cut sides of French bread loaf. Bake 40 minutes at 350 degrees, sprinkle with grated cheese and continue to bake until cheese melts and begins to bubble. Cut each hamburger half-loaf into 4 sections. *Serves 8 happy winners.*

ODIOUS ONION SANDWICHES

1½ cups chili sauce
¾ cup minced green pepper
Butter

16 slices toast, warm
2 large onions, thickly sliced
16 slices Swiss cheese

Simmer chili sauce and green pepper together in small saucepan for 10 minutes. Butter toast and cover each with 1 slice onion (Bermuda or yellow onions are best), a dollop of chili sauce mixture and a slab of Swiss cheese. (*) Toast under the broiler just until cheese melts. *Serves 8 (2 open-faced sandwiches apiece).*

CORNBREAD ARRIBA

Next to his *cerveza,* Pancho Villa loved this cornbread best:

1 package cornbread mix
1 egg, beaten
1½ cups milk
1 4-ounce can green chiles,
chopped and seeded

1 cup whole kernel corn
1 cup diced Jack cheese (or
any soft, mild cheese)

Set oven at 400 degrees. Blend cornbread mix with egg and milk. Pour half of batter in a greased 8-inch square baking pan. Sprinkle with chiles, then corn and cheese. Top with remaining batter. Bake for 35 minutes. Cut into 9 fat squares and serve to 3 or 4 with cold beer.

HIGH STAKES STEAK

2 pounds raw filet of beef,
ground twice
½ cup grated onion
⅓ cup red wine
2 tablespoons capers
2 teaspoons salt
2 small eggs, beaten slightly
¼ cup minced parsley

2 teaspoons seasoned pepper
2 teaspoons Worcestershire
sauce
½ cup sieved hard-cooked
egg
Buttered pumpernickel or rye
bread slices

Combine all ingredients with the exception of the sieved eggs and bread. Mix well and chill thoroughly in a tightly covered bowl for an hour. Turn out onto a platter and garnish with sieved egg and surround with buttered pumpernickel or rye bread slices. *Serves 8 generously.*

DEALER'S DUNK

Almost like a Cheddar fondue, but with some bonus points in the dunkables . . .

1 pint cream	*1 pound shrimp, cooked,*
2 teaspoons dry mustard	*cleaned and deveined*
1 tablespoon Worcestershire	*1 pound ground round,*
¼ teaspoon garlic powder	*seasoned and fried as meat*
6 cups shredded sharp	*balls*
Cheddar cheese	*1 loaf French bread, cut as for*
3 tablespoons flour	*fondue in 1-inch cubes*
Salt to taste	*6 bagels, cut ditto*

In an earthenware saucepan or casserole heat cream, mustard, Worcestershire and garlic until very hot but not boiling. Dredge cheese in flour and salt. Drop cheese, cup by cup, slowly into hot cream mixture. Stir with spoon until all cheese is melted. Put dunk over warmer and serve with shrimp, meatballs, French bread and bagels. Better supply skewers for easy spearing. *Serves 8.*

SMELLIES

Go home to Mother for a few days until the air clears . . .

½ cup olive oil	*¼ cup crumbled bleu cheese*
2 tablespoons lemon juice	*2 cups sliced red or yellow*
1 teaspoon salt	*onions*
Dash each pepper, paprika	*Sweet butter*
and sugar	*Pumpernickel or rye bread*

Mix oil, lemon juice and seasonings. Stir in cheese. Pour over onions and chill for 2–3 days. Serve with pumpernickel or rye that has been spread with sweet butter. *Serves 6.*

SALOON SPREAD

2 *pounds sharp Cheddar*
cheese, grated
1 *6-ounce can tomato paste*
1 *teaspoon garlic salt*

2 *tablespoons Worcestershire*
sauce
1 *12-ounce can beer*
Crackers or dark bread
rounds

Combine all ingredients to form smooth paste. If you can't find 12-ounce cans of brew, 2 8-ounce cans will do and you can nip on the rest, which isn't such a bad idea either. Serve with crackers or rounds of dark bread. *Serves 8–10.*

SHOWDOWN SHRIMP

2 *pounds shrimp, cleaned and*
cooked
1 *lemon, thinly sliced*
1 *small red onion, thinly*
sliced
½ *cup pitted black olives,*
sliced
2 *tablespoons chopped*
pimiento

½ *cup lemon juice*
¼ *cup olive oil*
1 *tablespoon garlic wine*
vinegar
⅛ *teaspoon garlic powder*
1 *bay leaf, crumbled*
1 *tablespoon cayenne*
Dash cracked black pepper
Salt to taste

Put shrimp in serving bowl and add lemon, onion, olives and pimiento. Toss. Mix together lemon juice, oil, vinegar and seasonings. Stir into shrimp and marinate for 12–24 hours. *Serves 6.*

CASINO CUCUMBERS WITH LOX

2 *pints sour cream*
1 *cucumber, thinly sliced*
1 *small red onion, thinly*
sliced

3 *tablespoons garlic wine*
vinegar
Salt and pepper to taste
Rye bread, thinly sliced
Lox, thinly sliced

Combine all ingredients and chill for 6 hours or more. Serve with thinly sliced rye and super-thin lox. The idea is that you put a slice of lox on a piece of rye, then load on the cucumber-sour cream mixture. *Serves 8.*

Two in the Bush

The season when ordinarily kindhearted business men
*   fill up their pockets with cartridges*
And go prowling around the woods in search of
*   caribous and partridges . . .*

OGDEN NASH

While they're counting their winnings, you'd better be dreaming up some more edibles, for when the mood strikes them you never know what they'll do next. If the poor demented souls have decided to make the next assembly a real outing with Nature, you now have your Size 7 in an even bigger snare. Without doubt, you'll be called upon to rustle up some grub—ordinarily they'd just ask you to "fix something to eat," but you know how it is when they go Hemingway all the way.

Any of the following will either pack well or can be reheated easily when the troops reach their ferny dell. But first, a bracer for Dutch courage:

LEIF ERIKSON'S GLUHWEIN

You can keep this warm in a thermos or just give the Boy Scouts the fixings and let them work at it, though ten to one has it that they'd forget the trivia and just tipple the bottle.

1 fifth California Burgundy
4 cinnamon sticks
1 teaspoon ground cinnamon
3 slices lemon peel, stuck with
*   cloves*

3 slices orange peel, stuck
*   with cloves*
1 teaspoon sugar

Blend all ingredients. (*) Heat thoroughly, but not to boiling.

Simmer gently for 5 minutes and serve in steaming hot mugs. *Serves 4.*

HUNTER'S LOAF

2 cups ground cooked cold
 meat (*beef, ham, veal or a
 combination; even chicken
 and chicken livers*)
2 pickles, finely chopped
2 tablespoons minced onion
3 tablespoons minced parsley
Dash Tabasco

2 hard-cooked eggs, chopped
1 tablespoon Worcestershire
Mayonnaise (*enough to bind
 together*)
Large loaf Vienna or Italian
 bread
Butter

Mix first 8 ingredients to a stiff paste. Cut heel off each end of loaf and scoop out the crumbs with a fork, leaving a shell of crust and about ½ inch of bread. Brush interior of loaf with a little melted butter and pack meat mixture in cavity very firmly. Return heels and wrap in foil. Should be refrigerated a couple of hours before slicing. *Serves 6 generously.*

BACKWOODS BEAN CHOWDER

2 onions, chopped
2 green peppers, chopped
2 sticks margarine
3 1-pound cans kidney beans,
 with juice
1 cup water

2 tablespoons Worcestershire
 sauce
1 teaspoon Tabasco
¾ pound Cheddar cheese,
 grated
Pumpernickel toast

Sauté onions and pepper in margarine until soft and glossy. Add remaining ingredients, except toast, and simmer until cheese melts and chowder is thick. (*) Serve with pumpernickel toast. *Serves 8.*

INSTEAD OFS

Instead of trout . . . instead of venison . . . instead of duck . . .

Butter
8 hot dog buns, partially split
8 frankfurters, partially split
8 narrow slices Swiss cheese

8 thin slices onion
8 pieces bacon, partially
    cooked

Butter the insides of the buns and set aside. Stuff each slit in the frankfurters with a slice of Swiss cheese and one of onion. Wrap partially cooked bacon around and secure with a toothpick. At this point you can wrap each frankfurter setup in foil, throw the buttered buns in a Baggie and let them take care of the rest. (*) The franks can be heated in the foil over a campfire and taken from the foil just at the end long enough to brown the bacon. *Serves 4.*

HEMINGWAY HAM SLICES

1 3-inch thick center slice
    ham
¼ cup prepared mustard

½ cup brown sugar
3 tablespoons honey

Preheat oven to 325 degrees. Slash edges of ham and bake in a shallow baking pan for 30 minutes. Combine remaining ingredients to make mustard glaze and baste with this frequently for another half hour or until crisp around edges. Slice across the grain when cool. This is not one of those sweet, gooey, clove-studded hams that most men hate—there's a real bite of authority to it. You can wrap the slices in foil and send them along with Curried Potato Salad or else tuck in a hefty loaf of bread and a pot of Wildman's Mustard for sandwiches. *Serves 8–10.*

WILDMAN'S MUSTARD

3 tablespoons dry mustard
2 tablespoons hot water
¼ teaspoon salt
1 teaspoon sugar

1 tablespoon olive oil
1 egg yolk
½ cup vinegar

Make a paste of mustard and water and stir in salt and sugar. Add oil and beat in egg yolk. Beat in vinegar to taste. *Serves 6.*

CURRIED POTATO SALAD

7 cups cubed cooked potatoes
½ cup diced green pepper
½ cup diced celery
2 cups diced hard-cooked egg
1¼ cups mayonnaise

2 teaspoons onion powder
3 tablespoons lemon juice
Salt and pepper to taste
Curry powder to taste (1–3
  tablespoons)

Mix all ingredients together until potatoes are coated. Chill 4–6 hours. *Serves 8.*

TAILGATERS

Practically guaranteed to bring them racing back to the nest:

⅓ cup butter
⅓ cup brown sugar
1 cup flour
½ cup chopped nuts
¼ cup granulated sugar

1 8-ounce package cream
  cheese, softened
1 egg
2 tablespoons milk
1 tablespoon lemon juice
½ teaspoon vanilla

Preheat oven to 350 degrees. Cream butter and brown sugar until fluffy. Add flour and nuts and blend until pebbly. Set aside 1 cup of crumbly mixture. Press remainder into 8-inch square pan and bake for 12–15 minutes. Beat sugar and cream cheese together until smooth. Add remaining ingredients and beat. Pour over baked crust, sprinkle with reserved crumbs. Bake for another 25–30 minutes. Cool and cut into 16 bars of creamy cheesecake. *Serves 8.*

So when they haul themselves up the driveway, dirty and disheveled, you can welcome them home with an honest smile. It's over for another year, old Red Plaid can return to the Goodwill bag and you're safe in the knowledge that you can still get to Bergdorf's before the sale is over.

**Gingham dogs and
calico cats**

6.

GINGHAM DOGS
AND
CALICO CATS

*A Collection of Battle-Tested Recipes
and Menus for Making Up*

*The gingham dog went "Bow-wow-wow"
And the calico cat replied "Mee-ow!"
The air was littered an hour or so,
With bits of gingham and calico.*

EUGENE FIELD

One thing's sure. Your mother won't tell you. Neither will the cool and efficient lady who mans the Bridal Registry. And the cavalier editors of those slick brides' magazines certainly wouldn't dream of it.

Nay, they'd have you believe that marriage is all sterling silver and guest lists, with your bridegroom serving only as a backdrop for your rose-point veil. How would they ever get rid of that five-year inventory of cedar chests if the truth were known? Not to mention their well-founded fear that we'd fast become a nation of spinsters.

The truth is that boys and girls are predestined to fight once in a while. Think back to the first grade when Billy Warnock tied knots in your jump rope. Or filled your favorite red galoshes with squiggly green bugs. Didn't you let him have a smart one across the shins with your lunch box? Though your retaliatory tactics may have become more covert, things haven't changed that much since your Buster Brown days.

If your husband is like Jack, who tries out his new 7-iron in Judy's tulip beds—or Ken, who insists on dragging 200 pounds of underwater camera equipment along on every trip—you'll need no suggestion from us on what to fight about. In moments of stress just being husband and wife seems enough provocation.

What we would suggest is that once the dust settles and peace has been negotiated, you set about preparing a feast to make him forget that your mother is coming for a month or that you ever told him about the dent in the new car. Light the candles and send the kids to Grandma's. Once your combat fatigue has worn off, hie yourself to the kitchen and attend to chilling the wine and sizzling the scampi. That half Nelson should cool down to a preoccupied bear hug.

BECKY'S SUMMIT SALAD

LAMB CHOPS MARINADE   ARMISTICE ARTICHOKES

LOVERS' LEMONADE PIE

LANCERS WINE

BECKY'S SUMMIT SALAD

4 small tomatoes, cut in small chunks	4 tablespoons mayonnaise
1 red onion, chopped	1 tablespoon minced parsley
Salt and pepper to taste	1 teaspoon or more curry powder

Toss and refrigerate tomatoes, onion and salt and pepper. Combine remaining ingredients. When ready to serve, spoon tomato-onion mixture into individual bowls and top with a glob of curry dressing. *Serves 2.*

LAMB CHOPS MARINADE

¼ cup olive oil
2 tablespoons garlic wine
  vinegar
2 teaspoons mustard
1 teaspoon rosemary
1 clove garlic, minced

¼ teaspoon ginger, ground
¾ teaspoon onion salt
1 teaspoon salt
¼ teaspoon coarsely ground
  pepper
4 thick loin lamb chops

Combine all ingredients except lamb chops. Marinate chops in marinade 4–5 hours. (*) Broil or grill approximately 20 minutes, turning once and basting as necessary. *Serves 2.*

ARMISTICE ARTICHOKES

2 globe artichokes, trimmed
Water, salt and salad oil
¼ cup olive oil
2 tablespoons garlic wine
  vinegar
1 shallot or 2 green onions,
  chopped

1 hard-cooked egg, sieved
1 tablespoon mustard
2 teaspoons minced parsley
1 teaspoon chopped chives
Dash each salt and pepper.

Cook the artichokes for 25 minutes in simmering water to which you have added a healthy dash of salt and about a tablespoon of salad oil. Combine remaining ingredients and serve as an accompanying dunk for the artichokes. *Serves 2.*

LOVERS' LEMONADE PIE

CRUST:

3 tablespoons butter, melted
1½ cups shredded coconut

Melt butter in skillet. Add coconut and stir over medium heat until golden brown. Press firmly into bottom and sides of a 9-inch pie pan. Let stand at room temperature until cool.

FILLING:

1 cup evaporated milk
1 envelope gelatin
¼ cup cold water
½ cup boiling water

⅔ cup sugar
1 6-ounce can frozen
 lemonade concentrate

Chill evaporated milk in ice tray until almost frozen around edges. In a large bowl, soften gelatin in cold water. Add boiling water and stir until all gelatin is dissolved. Add sugar and lemonade concentrate. Stir until lemonade thaws. Chill until very thick, but not set. Put ice cold milk into a cold 1-quart bowl. Whip at high speed until stiff. Fold into chilled gelatin-lemonade mixture. Spoon gently into coconut crust. Chill until firm—about 3 hours. *Serves 6.*

We suppose one of the nicest ways to coax a smile from your man is to serve him something he loves. If he dotes on liver and you're only lukewarm on the subject, you might try this. Even the staunchest anti-liver factions have succumbed to

LEMONY LIVER FOR THE LIVER LOVER
POSH POTATOES   SPINACH SALAD
INDIRA'S ENDEARING FRUIT

GAMAY BEAUJOLAIS

LEMONY LIVER FOR THE LIVER LOVER

8 strips bacon
1 pound beef or calves liver
Flour
Salt and pepper

3 tablespoons butter
2 tablespoons lemon juice
1 tablespoon minced parsley

Fry, drain and crumble bacon. Set aside. Dredge liver in flour that has been seasoned with salt and pepper. Fry quickly in same

pan in which bacon was cooked. Set liver aside and pour off fat
from pan. Heat butter in same skillet, stir in remaining ingredients along with crumbled bacon. Pour over warm liver slices.
Serves 2.

POSH POTATOES

Far above the pedestrian stuffed baked potato . . .

2 baking potatoes	*½ cup sour cream*
Salt and pepper to taste	*¼ cup finely diced celery*
3 tablespoons butter	*½ cup shredded Swiss cheese*
3 tablespoons milk	*Paprika*

Preheat oven to 450 degrees. Bake potatoes for 1 hour. Remove from oven and cut a long oval slit in the top of each. Scoop
out the innards and combine with all remaining ingredients except
paprika. Beat until light and fluffy. Return to potato shells and
continue heating at 450 degrees for 10 minutes. Sprinkle with
paprika. *Serves 2.*

SPINACH SALAD

1 bunch fresh raw spinach,	*4 strips bacon, fried and*
washed and drained	*crumbled*
1 hard-cooked egg, sieved	*Lawry's bottled Caesar*
2 green onions, sliced fine	*dressing*

Tear spinach into bite-size pieces. Add egg, green onion and
bacon; toss with Lawry's dressing. *Serves 2.*

INDIRA'S ENDEARING FRUIT

2 oranges	*½ cup snipped dates*
2 tablespoons shredded	*Dash bitters*
coconut	

Cut tops off oranges; remove pulp neatly and cut into small

pieces. Add remaining ingredients to pulp and toss. Return fruit mixture to orange shells and chill. *Serves 2.*

STUFFY STEAK

SEVILLIAN MUSHROOMS   BROCCOLI SOUFFLÉ

PRALINE PARFAIT

PINOT NOIR

STUFFY STEAK

1 pound round steak, ½ inch   ½ cup tomato juice
*   thick   2½ cups cooked wild rice*
Seasoned flour   ¼ cup chopped parsley
2 tablespoons butter   Shortening
¼ cup chopped onion   ¼ cup water
Salt and pepper to taste   ¼ cup red wine

Preheat oven to 350 degrees. Dredge meat in a little seasoned flour. Melt butter in a skillet and sauté onion until glossy. Stir in enough seasoned flour to thicken slightly and season with salt and pepper to taste. Add tomato juice; cook and stir. Add rice and parsley. Spread rice mixture on steak, roll and secure with skewers. (*) Brown meat in shortening; add liquids, cover and bake for 1½–2 hours. Sliced cold this makes a tremendous sandwich to sneak into his briefcase. *Serves 4.*

SEVILLIAN MUSHROOMS

¼ pound fresh mushrooms   1 tablespoon dry bread
1 tablespoon minced parsley   crumbs
¼ teaspoon fines herbes   1 tablespoon butter
¼ teaspoon onion powder   1 cup dry white wine
Dash each salt and pepper

Preheat oven to 350 degrees. Wash mushrooms and remove

stems. Chop stems and combine with parsley, fines herbes, onion powder, salt and pepper. Place mushroom caps in buttered baking dish and fill cavities with mushroom-herb mixture. Sprinkle with bread crumbs and dot with butter. Pour wine around bottom of mushrooms (*) and bake for 30 minutes. *Serves 2.*

BROCCOLI SOUFFLÉ

2 tablespoons butter
1 10-ounce package frozen
   chopped broccoli, cooked
   and drained
2 tablespoons flour

Salt to taste
½ cup milk, room
   temperature
¼ cup Parmesan cheese
4 eggs, separated

Preheat oven to 350 degrees. In a large skillet, add butter to broccoli and stir until melted. Set aside a handful of broccoli for garnish; add flour and salt to remaining broccoli. Stir and blend, adding milk gradually. Cook until thickened, stir in Parmesan. Remove from heat. (*) Beat egg yolks until thick and add broccoli mixture. Beat egg whites until stiff; fold into broccoli-egg yolk mixture. Bake in an ungreased soufflé dish for 25 minutes. Sprinkle top of soufflé with reserved broccoli and continue baking for 15 minutes. *Serves 4.*

PRALINE PARFAIT

2 cups dark brown sugar
1 tablespoon butter
⅓ cup boiling water

1 cup chopped pecans
Vanilla ice cream or coffee
   ice cream

Combine first four ingredients in saucepan and bring to a frantic boil. Continue to boil until thick and syrupy. Remove from heat, cool and store in refrigerator. Layer praline sauce with ice cream in tall parfait glasses and return to freezer until you're ready to serve. *Serves 2,* with extra sauce left over for the next battle.

AMNESTY ASPIC
BARBECUED BUTTERFLY LAMB
SNOW PEAS AND WATER CHESTNUTS   CURRIED PEACH HALF
SINFUL SUNDAE PIE
or
COFFEE COROT
CABERNET SAUVIGNON

AMNESTY ASPIC

An elegant appetizer to turn those swords into plowshares . . .

1 10-ounce can red consommé madrilene
¼ pound shrimp, cooked and cleaned
2 fresh mushrooms, sliced

Stir all ingredients together and chill. Serve in small consommé cups or bowls. *Serves 2.*

BARBECUED BUTTERFLY LAMB

1 5–6 pound leg of lamb,   *1 teaspoon salt*
  boned and butterflied   *¼ teaspoon cracked black*
1 small (8-ounce) carton sour   *pepper*
  cream   *Fat pinch each oregano, dried*
2 teaspoons MSG   *parsley, garlic powder*

Trim away the heavy paper-like fat from the outside of the lamb. This is referred to in more knowledgeable circles as the fell. Combine remaining ingredients and, leaving the lamb flat, smear marinade thickly on both sides of the butterfly. Cover and marinate 4–5 hours. (*) Grill over hot fire (or broil) 20 minutes on each side. Test for doneness as you go. *Serves 6.*

SNOW PEAS AND WATER CHESTNUTS

1 10-ounce package frozen Chinese pea pods
*2 water chestnuts, sliced thin (what you're going to do with all
the other chestnuts in the can is your own affair)*

Cook pea pods according to directions on the package. Drain
and toss with sliced water chestnuts. *Serves 2.*

CURRIED PEACH HALF

1 peach, peeled and halved   *2 tablespoons brown sugar*
2 teaspoons butter   ⅛ *teaspoon curry powder*

Preheat oven to 350 degrees. Dot cut sides of peach halves with
butter. Combine sugar and curry powder and sprinkle over
peaches. (*) Bake for 7–8 minutes. *Serves 2.*

SINFUL SUNDAE PIE

So good it's positively indelicate.

Vanilla wafers   *Dash salt*
1 cup evaporated milk   *2 pints vanilla ice cream,*
1 cup tiny marshmallows   *softened in refrigerator*
*1 6-ounce package chocolate
chips*

Line bottom and sides of greased 9-inch pie pan with whole
vanilla wafers. Combine milk, marshmallows, chocolate chips and
salt in saucepan. Cook and stir until blended and thick. Cool
slightly. Spoon one pint softened ice cream into wafer shell. Drizzle
half of sauce over ice cream; spoon on second pint of ice cream
and drizzle with remaining sauce. Return to freezer immediately.
Chill for 4 hours. *Serves 8–10.*

COFFEE COROT
(See Index)

FIELD MARSHAL'S FILET
ALMOND WILD RICE
TOSSED SALAD WITH ANCHOVY GARLIC DRESSING
RUM-RUNNER'S APPLE PIE
or
APPLE CHEESE PIE

CHAMBERTIN

FIELD MARSHAL'S FILET

1 3-pound filet of beef   *1 fat clove garlic, cut*
Pepper   *Salt*

Preheat oven to 375 degrees. Rub filet with pepper and cut clove of garlic. Place on rack and roast until meat thermometer registers 140 for rare or 150 for medium rare. If you like it any more well done than that, you don't deserve this heavenly cut. Sprinkle with salt about 10 minutes before removing from oven. *Serves 6.*

ALMOND WILD RICE

½ cup butter   *1 green onion, chopped (tops,*
1 cup fresh sliced mushrooms   *too)*
1 cup uncooked wild rice   *1 or 2 10-ounce cans beef*
½ cup slivered almonds   *consommé*

Preheat oven to 350 degrees. Melt butter in skillet and sauté mushrooms until golden. Add rice, almonds and onions. Cook over medium heat until rice is toasted, but watch for scorching. Add broth and heat to simmering. Transfer to a nice earthy serving dish and bake for an hour or so or until all the moisture is absorbed. It's a good idea to have that second can of broth on hand as insurance. Different brands of wild rice vary greatly and some will require more liquid. (*) Can be reheated at 375 degrees for 15 minutes. *Serves 6.*

ANCHOVY GARLIC DRESSING

1 can anchovy filets plus oil
⅔ cup olive oil
⅓ cup wine vinegar
1 teaspoon Worcestershire
Pinch each basil, thyme and
   oregano

⅛ teaspoon garlic powder
½ onion, sliced
Salt and pepper to taste
2 teaspoons catsup

Throw it all in a blender and give it a whirl. *Makes 1 cup dressing.*

RUM-RUNNER'S APPLE PIE

PIECRUST FOR A 2-CRUST 9-INCH PIE

5–6 cups sliced fresh cooking
   apples (*Jonathans*)
¼ cup flour
1½ cups brown sugar, firmly
   packed

1½ teaspoons cinnamon
Dash salt
4 tablespoons butter
3 tablespoons rum

Preheat oven to 425 degrees. Fit one crust into bottom of pie plate. Line bottom of crust with layer of sliced apples. Combine flour, brown sugar, cinnamon and salt. Sprinkle a portion of this over the apple slices and dot with butter. Repeat this layering process until you run out; be sure the apple slices are mounded high in the center. Fit top crust over all and trim and flute. Cut slits for steam vents and slip into the oven for 50 suspenseful minutes. When pie is done and cooling, pour rum through slits. *Serves 6 generously.*

APPLE CHEESE PIE

1 9-inch piecrust
¼ cup flour
1½ cups sugar
1½ teaspoons cinnamon

5–6 cups tart cooking apples,
   sliced thin
4 tablespoons butter
½ cup Cheddar cheese,
   grated

TOPPING:

½ cup brown sugar, firmly   1 ¼ cups flour
   packed   ½ cup butter

Powdered sugar

Preheat oven to 400 degrees. Line pie plate with crust and set aside. Combine flour, sugar and cinnamon. Line bottom of crust with layer of sliced apples and sprinkle some of flour-sugar mixture over the slices; dot with some butter. Repeat layering process until you run out of apples. Scatter grated cheese over apples. Combine topping ingredients and stir until crumbly. Sprinkle over apples and layer of cheese. Bake 40 minutes or until apples are tender when jabbed with a fork. When cool, dust with powdered sugar. *Serves 6.*

PETULANT PAUL'S CRAB CHABLIS

WHITE RICE   PRESERVED KUMQUATS

TOSSED SALAD   LEMON-OIL DRESSING

CHILLY CHEESE TORTE

CHABLIS

PETULANT PAUL'S CRAB CHABLIS

4 tablespoons butter   1 pound fresh crabmeat
4 tablespoons flour   1 teaspoon fresh ground
1 cup milk, room temperature   pepper
½ cup Chablis   Salt, paprika and cayenne to
1 cup grated Cheddar or   taste
   Tillamook cheese   ⅓ cup buttered bread crumbs
10 medium mushrooms, sliced
   and sautéed in butter

Preheat oven to 350 degrees. Melt butter in a large skillet and add flour. Slowly add milk and cook and stir until thick. Add

Chablis, cheese and mushrooms. Blend in crabmeat and seasonings. Transfer to serving casserole, sprinkle top with bread crumbs and bake for 25 minutes or until golden and bubbly. (*) *Serves 4.*

LEMON-OIL DRESSING

½ *cup olive oil*
¼ *cup lemon juice*
1 *teaspoon salt*

½ *teaspoon coarse ground pepper*

Combine, shake and serve tossed with crisp chilled greens and a handful of capers. *Makes ¾ cup dressing.*

CHILLY CHEESE TORTE

CRUST:

1 *cup cornflake crumbs*
⅓ *cup margarine, softened*
2 *tablespoons sugar*

FILLING:

2 *8-ounce packages cream cheese, very soft*
2 *cups light Karo syrup*
2 *cups milk*

2 *teaspoons vanilla*
1 *12-ounce jar raspberry or strawberry preserves*

Combine cornflake crumbs, margarine and sugar. Press into bottom of 9-inch spring form pan. Chill. Muddle the cream cheese and Karo around together until well blended and then add milk and vanilla, slowly, beating well as you go. Pour over crumbs and freeze for several hours. When ready to serve, remove sides of pan and smear the fruit preserves over the torte. This must be returned to the freezer between servings. *Makes 12 rich, rich wedges.*

So you see what *is* different is that fighting with big boys can be fun, mostly because you get to make up. Saying you're sorry will always be as hard as it was back in the first grade, but now you can nuzzle his neck a little. Young Billy Warnock never would have stood still for that.

Party politics

7.

PARTY
POLITICS

There's no way around the fact that giving a party is a lot of work and that in the morning you're left with new rings on your lowboy and a devastating scorch on the Aubusson. We really prefer a quiet evening with six or eight friends, embellished by a languorous cocktail hour and a fattening dinner.

But the time always comes when our men balk at our lazy little get-togethers and vote for a good old-fashioned gala. Then we just sigh resignedly and get busy ironing those two dozen linen napkins that have been happily mildewing in the laundry basket since the last bash.

Actually, despite the work involved, we've found that there's no better way to make points with your prince consort than to allow him to host the party of the season. Look what it did for Truman Capote.

So once a year it is worth the effort to shine up the house, go in hock to the grocer and prepare yourself for an onslaught of the Visigoths. You'll find that on the evening of the party he'll strut around, showing off his own private kingdom with all the pride of a boy with the best Flexi-Flyer on the block.

Since it's easier to get yourself in gear for one of these grisly events if you have some kind of theme in mind, you'll find here ten party ideas that, for better or for worse, should get you through a decade of entertaining. After that you're on your own.

Curry Party

Men may be content to let the ladies grapple with the mundane kitchen chores night after night, but when it comes to culinary pyrotechnics they're right there to take the bows. Almost every man we've ever known has one whopper of a recipe that he calls his own. We have one friend—a photographer—who falls into this category. He is almost as famous for his annual Christmas Curry Party as he is for his splendid photographs. Invitations to his party are as coveted as a bid to an Onassis cruise. In fact, his formidable curry has become such a standard that he has never had to bother to expand his epicurean repertoire and yet he enjoys a reputation as a classic chef.

We finally wheedled the recipe for this laudable curry from him and present it to you here. Curry is really marvelous party fare, for the food itself is so handsome that decorations are superfluous. Set a buffet on a batik, Paisley or Madras tablecloth, use lots of brass and copper and the curry's colorful condiments, served in small individual bowls, will serve as a centerpiece.

An Indian-inspired dinner gives the hostess a perfect opportunity to greet her guests in the most exotic fashions. If you have a caftan, a djellaba or a sari this is the ideal time to wear it. If you really want to be authentic and think you can get away with it, glue a Woolworth jewel in the middle of your forehead.

A refreshing change from the usual ham and/or roast beef buffet fare, curry is nearly as simple to prepare and requires only a short period of Zen-like concentration to see it through. Some caution is in order, however, for curry, like politics, brings out the most violent reactions in people. There is no tolerant middle ground—only curry lovers and curry haters—so be sure to make up your guest list carefully.

In India the guests eat curry with their fingers, using the first three fingers of their right hands as a kind of scoop. Your guests would probably wonder if you had regressed to high chair days if you tried to introduce this authentic refinement to your party, so you'd better stick to knives and forks. As to seating guests, if sit-down room is at a premium let them recline exotically on the floor—perhaps on grass matting—around a low coffee table.

The number of condiments that accompany your curry is a Middle-Eastern status symbol. According to legend, the wealth of an Indian maharajah was judged by the number of slaves he owned. At a palace dinner each condiment or sambal was carried to the table by a different slave. Thus, the more sambals, the more boys to carry them and the more wealth they represented. Today curry dinners are still referred to as "six boy curry" or "ten boy curry," depending on the number of sambals presented. So if you want the Joneses to have to try to keep up with you, be extravagant with your condiments.

There are any number of sambals from which to choose so don't be stingy. You could have any of the following:

Toasted salted coconut	*Grated lemon rind*
Chopped peanuts or cashews	*Chutney (Major Grey's is ex-*
Diced candied ginger	*cellent)*
Mandarin orange segments	*Raisins plumped in wine*
Chopped hard-cooked eggs	*Grated lime rind*
Banana chips	*Sliced black olives*
Chopped onions	*Crumbled cooked bacon*
Melon balls	*Chopped cucumber*
Chopped green pepper	*Chopped tomato*
Chopped green chiles	*Chopped dates*

And now, bring on the curry . . .

JAY THOMPSON'S WORLD RENOWNED CURRY

RICE

BAKED BANANAS

PURIS

CANTALOUPE WITH RASPBERRY ICE

BEER or CHABLIS

JAY THOMPSON'S WORLD RENOWNED CURRY

6 tablespoons butter
6 tablespoons flour
3½ cups milk which has been heated (but not boiled) for 15 minutes with
1 can shredded coconut (save coconut, toast and salt for sambals)
1 large onion, diced
1½ teaspoons ground pepper
2 teaspoons salt
2 teaspoons paprika

1½ teaspoons powdered ginger
4–6 tablespoons good Indian Curry powder, imported (Jay recommends P. Ventcachellum or Sun Brand)
Water
1–2 tablespoons domestic curry powder
3 pounds fresh cleaned and cooked medium shrimp

Melt butter over low heat. Add flour and stir to form a smooth paste. Add the coconut-flavored milk and heat until thick, stirring all the while. Add the onion and the remaining spices except the curry. Make a paste of the imported curry powder with a little warm water and add it a tablespoon at a time to the mixture, tasting after each addition. When the heat of the curry sauce suits you, add the domestic curry powder, which will add a smooth sweetness to the mixture. Finally, add the shrimp and simmer lightly for 5 minutes. Cool and refrigerate overnight.(*) Be sure to make your curry at least 12 hours before you plan to serve it as it should have time for the flavors to marry.

Reheat curry *slowly* about an hour before serving over rice. *Serves 8–10.*

RICE

(See Index)

BAKED BANANAS

8 bananas
Lemon juice

Bake the bananas in their skins for 20 minutes at 350 degrees. Peel them and serve hot with a squeeze of lemon juice. *Serves 8.*

PURIS

2 cups whole wheat flour
2 teaspoons baking powder
1 teaspoon salt

2 tablespoons oil
1 cup cold water
Salad oil

Mix the flour, baking powder, salt, oil and water. (*) Roll into about 15 1½–2-inch balls. Now roll each ball into a ⅛-inch thick circle. Pour 2 inches of salad oil into a skillet or deep fat fryer. Heat the oil to about 380 degrees on a deep fat thermometer. Drop in the dough circles, one at a time, holding under the fat with the tip of a wooden spoon until puffy and bubbly. Cook until brown, turning once and drain on paper towel. Keep warm in a 175 degree oven. When they are all done pile on a plate and serve. *Makes 15.*

CANTALOUPE WITH RASPBERRY ICE

4 cantaloupes
1 quart raspberry ice

Cut cantaloupes in half and hollow out the centers, discarding seeds. Fill each hollow with raspberry ice and serve chilled. *Serves 8.*

St. Valentine's Day Massacre

It isn't everyone who gets invited to a massacre and lives to tell about it.

Your friends will, though, if you'll include them in your guest list for a St. Valentine's Day Massacre. We weren't around in Chicago's heyday either, but we've heard sufficient stories at our daddies' gnarled old knees to keep Flaming Youth burning in our hearts for a lot of years to come. There's enough ribaldry connected with the Jazz Age and Prohibition to make even World War II babies get all weepy with nostalgia.

But rather than giving an ordinary Prohibition or Roaring Twenties party, last year we combined forces and staged a St. Valentine's Day Massacre. Our invitations went out a couple of weeks before Valentine's Day in the macabre form of black ruffled hearts.

If you're a purist you'll recall that the 1929 massacre took place in a garage on Chicago's North Side and you'll set about seeing what miracles can be wrought to warm up the inside of your garage. If yours is a mélange like ours, though, the walls are probably lined with boxes of Gro-Rite and an impenetrable pool of thick black sludge graces the middle of the floor. Sadly, this spells work, and parties are enough work without peering around for more. Besides, any hostess is allowed plenty of license; your guests won't say a word about authenticity if you doll up your living room and dining room to look like a South Side speakeasy.

Scatter small intimate tables for four or six about the living room, with the only lights being low guttering candles on each table. Place cards can be sympathy cards you've filched from the florist. A prop rental establishment is the place to find a squatty-legged iron bathtub in which you can serve a lethal gin punch or whatever form of bootleg poison you've decided on. Serve the drinks in coffee cups for a genuine Prohibition touch, but it's a good idea to have glasses on hand for those serious drinkers who like to see what it is they're consuming.

The current return to art from the thirties and forties should make it easy enough for you to pick up several posters of a campy nature that can be tacked up strategically. Music is no problem—a stack of Lester Lanin and Ernie Heckscher albums on the Gramophone ought to send you and your guests right back to the days of the big bands. While you're at it, investigate any possibilities for renting or buying old films from the thirties. Douse the lights after dinner and bring on an old Humphrey Bogart-John Garfield shoot-'em-up.

Most men seem to revert to the obdurate mule-like creatures that they are when the word costume is spoken above a whisper. Luckily, this is one party where the prospect of dressing for the occasion practically transports them. Just about anything reminiscent of the era of flappers and dandies will do for both of you. If you have a fringed dress still hanging around from the early 1960s, haul it out. Search through your mother's old clothes—don't you remember that skinny green rayon dress trimmed in maribou that you used to play dress-up in? Failing this, you can do what we did and comb the local Salvation Army thrift shop. You'll be amazed at some of the moldering boas and beaded headbands you'll find there among the bins of oversized saddle shoes and old Morris chairs. For the men, again the thrift shop is about the only place they'll find that double-breasted pinstriped suit in just the right shade of electric blue gabardine. A wide hand-painted tie, a pretentious watch chain and a roll-brim Fedora should complete the Frank Nitty aura.

If you live in a fairly large city, there are services that will rent you groaning old Cadillac or La Salle hearses to pick up your guests. Once they've all arrived and are gathered 'round the bathtub, you can see to the:

CAPONE'S COW

MOLL'S MUSHROOMS   O'BANNION'S BREAD

SYNDICATE SALAD

THE DUTCHMAN'S TORTE

BORDEAUX

When we trotted home (almost literally) with this enormous

piece of meat, our husbands' only comment was that that was not meat, woman, but Cow. Herein, our recipe for

CAPONE'S COW

1 enormous piece top round steak, 7–8 pounds and 3 inches thick
Unseasoned meat tenderizer
1 cup olive oil
1 cup red wine
¼ cup garlic wine vinegar
1 teaspoon salt

Lots of cracked black pepper —at least 1 teaspoon
¼ teaspoon garlic powder
1 teaspoon oregano
1 teaspoon basil
1 medium onion, sliced very thin or grated

Trim any excess fat away from steak. Pierce all over at 2-inch intervals and sprinkle on meat tenderizer generously. Allow to stand at room temperature for 30 minutes. Combine all remaining ingredients in a large flat pan, plop in the steak, cover and refrigerate for at least 12 hours. Turn every few hours or whenever you can remember. The trick is to put Cow (by now you'll be getting attached to the beast) on the grill close to a hot fire just after the guests arrive. Turn only once, but baste often with the marinade. It should take about 45 minutes for rare, an hour for medium. Slice it daintily like Chateaubriand—it's beautifully charred on the outside and fairly mooing inside. The joy of it is that your guests have to smell that gorgeous Cow cooking all during cocktails and by the time you're finally ready to serve, they're all so primed by the prospect that anything would taste like filet. *Serves 8.*

Our friend Jessica looks upon mushrooms as suspicious little growths that should have been left in the woods. But even she craves these:

MOLL'S MUSHROOMS

3 pounds medium-sized mushrooms
½ pound butter

1 teaspoon paprika
⅛–¼ teaspoon garlic powder
½ teaspoon fresh dill weed

Wash and trim mushrooms. Do not peel. Allow to drain on a

paper towel. In a large heavy skillet, melt butter slowly and add seasonings. Keep butter just warm for about 5 minutes while seasonings intermingle. Add mushrooms and sauté gently for about 10 minutes or until tender. *Serves 8.*

O'BANNION'S BREAD

Mrs. O'Bannion sent along a batch to the flower shop every day:

1 dozen hard French rolls (smallish)	3 teaspoons Dijon mustard
1½ cubes softened butter (¾ cup)	2 tablespoons parsley flakes
	3 tablespoons chopped chives
	Parmesan cheese

Split the rolls and set aside. Mix remaining ingredients with the exception of the cheese and spread on the cut surface of the rolls. Sprinkle heavily with grated Parmesan cheese. Place close together on a cookie sheet, cover with foil (*) and bake at 375 degrees for 15 minutes. Remove foil and bake another 5–7 minutes or until crispy and slightly brown on top. *Serves 8.*

SYNDICATE SALAD

2–3 heads romaine, torn in bite-size pieces	1–2 large avocados, peeled and thinly sliced
1 can water chestnuts, sliced thin	Oil and vinegar dressing

Combine greens, water chestnuts and sliced avocado. Toss in chilled salad bowl with your favorite oil and vinegar dressing. *Serves 8.*

THE DUTCHMAN'S TORTE

About 30 macaroons or chocolate cookies	1 quart chocolate ice cream, softened
1 quart coffee ice cream, softened	1 dozen 5-cent Butter Brickle candy bars (or any other that resembles English toffee)
Canned chocolate sauce	

Crush macaroons and place half of them on the bottom of a

9-inch spring form pan. Smear on coffee ice cream, drizzle with some chocolate sauce. Layer on the remaining cookie crumbs, the chocolate ice cream, a little more chocolate sauce. Top with crushed English toffee candy. Freeze at least 6 hours. *Serves 8.*

Tiptoe Through the Tulips Smorrebrod Party

After a winter's worth of dreary days, even the most stalwart soul becomes giddy on the first day of spring. Should you be struck down by an especially virulent case of spring fever why enjoy it alone—have a party and start an epidemic.

However, unless you live in an area blessed by singularly dependable weather, plan to have your party in the late spring. Barring a downpour, this is one party that should be held outside. And don't despair if outside for you means an apartment terrace, for there are plenty of things you can do to make even a big city balcony as spring-like as a Victorian gazebo. The lack of a real garden poses no problem for it's simple enough to plant a paper one. Use bowers of crepe paper flowers—some wired to sticks and planted in the ground or a planter box—to decorate your patio or terrace.

Your smørrebrød table will add another touch of spring if you cover it in green burlap and make a centerpiece of potted tulips, daffodils and hyacinths. After the party each of your guests can take home a pot of flowers as a favor. Another spring spread might reside on a table covered in yellow and white striped denim decorated with baskets spilling over heaps of fresh daisies.

A single tulip sent by the florist should accompany your invitation to the party. And on the invitation ask everyone to come equipped with a homemade kite for a kite-flying contest. Then pray that the day of the party doesn't dawn with a deadly calm.

Kite-flying will keep the men busy figuring out stress factors and aerodynamic lift while you set out the feast. If you have the room and think your friends have the inclination, croquet is also a good game for a spring party. As a matter of fact, croquet is having a vast resurgence with the smart set and there's nothing wrong with being thought a pacesetter in your province.

If you are going to offer games and contests then you'd better be prepared to offer prizes too. Garden gloves, trowels, seed packets, bulbs and—for the losers—crabgrass killer, are all appropriate prizes. If you really feel generous you might give your kite-fliers prizes for the most beautiful, the most original and so forth.

Plan to buy a spanking new wheelbarrow and spray it a bright color ready for the day of the party when it will hold crushed ice and bottles of chilled May wine.

Our menu for tiptoeing through the tulips is one with a Danish flavor, in fact it was inspired by Denmark's own garden of enchantment, the Tivoli.

Spring Smørrebrød

PRINCELY POTATO SALAD

HAMLET'S HAPPINESS   GREAT DANE SANDWICH

OSCAR'S OYSTER SANDWICH   LUSCIOUS LOBSTER SANDWICH

THE HANS CHRISTIAN ANDERSEN SANDWICH

STRAWBERRIES IN MAY WINE

or

DANISH BEER

PRINCELY POTATO SALAD

6 cups cold, sliced cooked potatoes (2½ pounds)	1½ teaspoons salt
1 cup minced onions	¼ teaspoon pepper
½ cup finely chopped celery	¼ pound salami, slivered
¼ cup finely chopped parsley	4 hard-cooked eggs, sliced
1½ teaspoons prepared mustard	1½ cups mayonnaise
	Lettuce
	Chopped chives

Toss together the potatoes, onions, celery, parsley, mustard and salt and pepper until well mixed. Add slivered salami (this is most easily done with kitchen shears—if you've ever been able to secure a pair of scissors for kitchen use alone), eggs, and mayonnaise. You may want to use more mayonnaise if you like your salad damper. Stir all together and chill until ready to serve. Spoon onto lettuce leaves in a bowl. Garnish with chopped chives. *Serves 12.*

Before you begin to assemble the smørrebrød perhaps we should fill you in a bit on the impression these delightful Danish sandwiches left on us when we first met up with them in their native land. First, each sandwich should be not only delicious to the taste but a delight to the eye as well. In addition to carefully garnishing each individual sandwich, the Danes add additional color to their platters with lemon or lime wedges, large bunches of watercress, gherkins cut into fancy shapes, plum tomatoes and marinated artichoke hearts and nests of lettuce filled with potato salad. Draft all of your friends' best silver, wooden and china platters to use for bringing your smørrebrød to your hunger-crazed guests. Obviously this is no mere sandwich—it's a major studio production. And it requires the use of a knife and fork to cope with its generous proportions.

You must select the breads on which to build these culinary masterpieces as carefully as Rembrandt selected his canvas. No soggy white bread is allowed here. Only whole grain wheat, pumpernickel, sour rye, Danish rye (called rugbrød) or *very close grained* white are fine enough to support these works of art. The breads you select should be very thinly sliced—about one-quarter of an inch.

The butter with which you spread the bread is equally important. It should be unsalted and should be creamed until it is the color of pale sunshine. Once it is creamed, divide it into several portions and add a pinch of curry to one portion, mustard to another, chives to another and horseradish to yet another.

Any of the following sandwiches can be made the morning of the party. Just put the sandwiches on a cookie sheet, cover with plastic wrap or foil and stow in the refrigerator.

Now that the bread and butter are all set, here's the rest of the story.

HAMLET'S HAPPINESS

No one could be melancholy after a taste of this sandwich!

2 cans beef consommé
24 thinly sliced pieces roast beef
12 slices black pumpernickel
Horseradish butter

3 or 4 hard-cooked eggs
3 or 4 tomatoes, sliced
1 cucumber, peeled and sliced
1 green pepper, cut in diamonds or other shapes

Chill consommé until slightly thickened. Place 2 roast beef slices on a piece of pumpernickel lavishly spread with horseradish butter and top with other ingredients attractively arranged. Put on a cookie sheet and chill 20 minutes. Spoon consommé over sandwiches to cover completely. Chill about 30 minutes. *Serves 12.*

GREAT DANE SANDWICH

6 hard-cooked eggs
6 ounces bleu cheese
½ cup mayonnaise
¾ teaspoon lemon juice
1½ teaspoons prepared mustard
¾ teaspoon sugar

¾ teaspoon reconstituted instant onion
Salt and pepper
12 slices close-grained whole wheat bread
Chive butter
24 slices Danish ham

Finely dice hard-cooked eggs. Combine diced eggs, crumbled bleu cheese, mayonnaise, lemon juice, mustard, sugar and reconstituted instant onion. Add salt and pepper to taste. Spread bread with soft chive butter. Place 2 slices of ham on each piece of bread. Spoon egg mixture onto center of each sandwich. *Makes 12 open-faced sandwiches.*

OSCAR'S OYSTER SANDWICH

3 hard-cooked eggs
2 green peppers
12 slices Danish rye bread

Onion-parsley butter
3 (3⅔ ounce) cans smoked
oysters, chilled

Cut 24 lengthwise strips of egg white ¼ inch wide. Cut pepper into 24 long strips. Butter bread with onion-parsley butter. Chop egg yolks very fine. Arrange oysters on bread and sprinkle with chopped egg yolk. Arrange green pepper and egg strips prettily on top. *Makes 12 open-faced sandwiches.*

LUSCIOUS LOBSTER SALAD SANDWICH

2 cans asparagus spears (reserve a few spears for garnish)
4 cans (4½ ounce) lobster
1 cup mayonnaise
3 tablespoons tarragon vinegar

½ teaspoon salt
12 lettuce leaves
Curry butter
12 slices thinly cut French
bread
12 lemon slices

Cut asparagus into ½-inch chunks. Mix lobster, chopped asparagus, mayonnaise, vinegar and salt. Place lettuce leaf on each piece of curry buttered bread and spread with mixture. Garnish with asparagus tips and a slice of lemon. *Makes 12 open-faced sandwiches.*

THE HANS CHRISTIAN ANDERSEN SANDWICH

This is an adaptation of the most popular sandwich served at Oscar Davidson's, the famed Copenhagen restaurant with the mile-long menu.

24 slices bacon, fried crisp
12 slices Danish rye
Sweet butter

2 cans (4½ ounce) liver pâté
24 thin slices tomato
Horseradish

Place 2 rows of bacon on top of the slices of rye bread, which you have spread with sweet butter. Place a sliver of liver pâté on one row and 2 slices of tomato across the other. Top the tomato slices with a smidgen of horseradish. This is the only sandwich that should be assembled just before the party, since you don't want the bacon to become stiff and ugly. Serve immediately. *Serves 12.*

STRAWBERRIES IN MAY WINE

Place several hulled strawberries in the bottom of a champagne glass and fill with May wine.

Assembling all of these sandwiches is no small chore so if you're wise you'll enlist the aid of a friend or else get some professional help. Four hands can make light work of this party and once you've seen your smørrebrød displayed in all its glory you'll forget the drudgery of dicing hard-cooked eggs and cutting green pepper in tiny decorative shapes—you'll just be reassured that spring will be pretty great this year.

The Ides of April

While Caesar may have feared the Ides of March, our twentieth-century husbands are more likely to side with Eliot's contention that April is the cruelest month. For April brings those despicably cheerful IRS men toting imitation cowhide briefcases jam-packed with balance sheets, recriminations and when it's all over—outright poverty.

This horror-fraught purge is enough to undermine anyone's social calendar but now is not the time to sit about fondling your fading Neiman Marcus clothes. The effective way to take your mind off your dwindling bank account is to plan a party.

Gather together your surviving down-and-outers for an evening amalgam of the very tacky and the very elegant at an Income Tax Party. The whole mood of this party should be that of a gay group of paupers, making do with their last tiaras just a throw away from the pawn shop. You may be eating beans, but at least you're doing it on the most translucent of Limoges.

Your invitations can be crudely torn scraps of butcher paper or foolscap, but worded in High Emily Post. Or you might purchase pre-worded formal invitations with spaces allowed for host, etc. In the lower right-hand corner you can indicate dress by something vague like Black Tie and Tennis Shoes. If you trust your friends, send one of your personal checks payable to Mr. and Mrs. So and So, One Income Tax Party. Your name and address will already be on the printed check so all you need do is add the date and time and R.S.V.P. With this type of invitation, they'll probably telephone to reply, so you can explain then that the dress is whatever they have left after they've paid their taxes. Any getup that indicates your recent candidacy for Skid Row will be fine, as long as you make it clear that you're still clinging to the vestiges of your lost wealth with fierce Scott Fitzgerald pride. Your really high-bracket friends may have to take a poor-but-proud hint from Scarlett O'Hara's book and wrench down the velvet portieres for swaddling, but for most a tuxedo and go-aheads or morning clothes and a T-shirt will do. Even a barrel will suffice if you think you can count on no peeking. Women have the most room for imagination—one of our friends came decked out in pink lace and dirty tennies; another with an old underskirt draped around her shoulders, calling it her "summer ermine." If you're really ingenious, you can fashion a chic new paper mini-dress out of an old Goodwill bag, set off by piles of fake diamonds from the five and dime.

Make a tablecloth of old newspapers taped together (or more Goodwill bags if you can abide that garish yellow they've adopted) but set it with your haughtiest china and crystal, heaviest of sterling. Strew phony gold coins along the table; for place card favors, find some inexpensive tin cups while you're at the dime store selecting your diamonds. Fill the cups with pencils and paint a guest's name on each. Or if you *really* have a lot of poor friends and you're serving a buffet in lieu of a sit-down affair, we recommend theft. Sidle into the bank early in March and slip a gross of 1040 forms into your reticule while no one's looking. Then stop at the dime store again on your way home and pick up a cheap lap tray for each guest. Collage the 1040 forms to the trays by applying first a coat of quick-dry clear varnish or shellac to the tray, slapping on enough tax forms to cover the visible surfaces and allowing to dry for a couple of hours. Cover the whole business with another coat of varnish and let dry for a couple of days. With the black and white trays, bright "in the red" napkins would be effective.

You'll be bucking a head wind in striving for enthusiastic party spirit on this particular night, so be ready to greet your guests with plenty of liquid placebos—after all, what's the first thing a Skid Row nabob spends his last nickel on?

Make no apologies as you serve up this simple fare:

BETTER DAYS BEANS

MISER'S MUSTARD BREAD

TOSSED SALAD   UPPER BRACKET BEER DRESSING

DEBTOR'S DESSERT

BEER

BETTER DAYS BEANS

1 bunch green onions, chopped
2 green peppers, chopped
3 tablespoons olive oil
2 pounds ground round
Salt and pepper

5–6 small tomatoes, chopped
3 cups Burgundy wine
3 29-ounce cans dark red kidney beans, drained

Sauté onions and green pepper in the olive oil until soft and shiny. Add the ground round and push it around until brown and crumbly; season to taste. Stir in the fresh chopped tomatoes and wine; simmer a moment. Add beans, stir gently and shove it, en casserole, in a 350 degree oven for something upward of 20 minutes—just so it's good and hot all the way through. *Serves 8 generously.*

MISER'S MUSTARD BREAD

1 dozen sourdough French rolls
1 stick margarine (you can't afford butter!)
3 tablespoons Dijon mustard
1 tablespoon poppy seeds

Split the rolls, make a smooth paste of the softened margarine and mustard. Smear lavishly over cut sides of the French rolls and sprinkle with poppy seeds. Bake on a cookie sheet at 350 degrees for 15 minutes or so until hot and crispy. *Serves 8 generously.*

UPPER BRACKET BEER DRESSING

½ cup olive oil
¼ teaspoon salt
Dash seasoned pepper
⅛ teaspoon garlic powder
3 tablespoons lemon juice
1 teaspoon sugar
¼ cup flat beer
1 teaspoon paprika

Combine and blend until smooth. Chill. Toss with chilled, crisp greens and serve. Makes 1 cup. *Serves 8.*

DEBTOR'S DESSERT

Debtor's Dessert is, in reality, a euphemism for our loyal standby, Fruit and Cheese. But you might try the following combinations for a change:

Cheeses: Petit Suisse, Brie, Port du Salut, Fontina, Stilton

Fruit: Apples, pears, peaches, fresh figs, strawberries and green grapes.

Serve cheese at room temperature and the fruit bowl icy cold. Thin, tasteless soda crackers are considered the best accompaniment along with a little sweet butter.

Bastille Day Parties

When the American holidays begin to seem like pallid excuses for a party you'll have to become more international in scope. One of the best foreign holidays to adopt is July 14—French Bastille Day. Despite our tepid political relations with the French of late, there is no reason to miss this delightful occasion. Bastille Day was certainly not a jolly event when it occurred, but its anniversary is celebrated in France in much the same manner as our Fourth of July. Since Bastille Day is commemorated not only in France but in all the French possessions, we thought you should have your choice of two very different celebrations: Parisian Bastille Day and Tahitian Bastille Day.

Parisian Bastille Day

The invitations for this party could be written with a felt pen on French newspapers (you should be able to get these at a large newspaper stand or bookstore). Of course you'll set your table on red and white checked cloths with candles stuck in wine bottles. If you're very ambitious (or better yet, if your husband is) construct a kiosk out of cardboard and plaster it with French travel posters to give the party a nice Left Bank touch.

In keeping with the French theme you might ask any of your friends who are Sunday painters to bring samples of their work and set up a Montmartre gallery in your living room. Put some French records (Charles Aznavour, Edith Piaf, Jacques Brel, Maurice Chevalier) on your hi-fi for soft background music. You can finish off the evening with a bang if you've been foresighted enough to stash away some of your Fourth of July fireworks for the occasion.

Since Bastille Day honors the equality of all Frenchmen we

suggest a menu that cuts across class distinctions. From the sturdy peasant stock of Marseille comes the aromatic Bouillabaisse. The finest tradition of French haute cuisine contributes the Profiterolles Chantilly and, sustaining the entire meal are the two staffs of life for all classes—French bread and wine.

BOUILLABAISSE
ROMAINE AND ENDIVE SALAD
FRENCH BREAD
PROFITEROLLES CHANTILLY

WHITE BURGUNDY

BOUILLABAISSE

1 carrot, chopped
1 clove garlic, crushed
2 onions, chopped
White part of 2 leeks, chopped
½ cup olive oil
3 pounds assorted white fish
2 large tomatoes, chopped
1 bay leaf
2 cups water
2 teaspoons salt

1 lobster, cut in small pieces
1 pound shrimp, shelled and cleaned
1 dozen oysters or clams in the shells, scrubbed
Few grains powdered saffron
1 cup white wine
Pepper
Chopped parsley

In a large kettle or casserole cook the carrot, garlic, onions and leeks in olive oil until golden. Add the fish (cut in 3-inch pieces), tomatoes, bay leaf, water and salt. Bring to a boil and simmer for 20 minutes. Add the lobster and cook for 10 minutes. Add the shrimp, oysters or clams, saffron, wine and pepper to taste; cook for 10 more minutes. Add parsley and correct the seasoning (soup should be spicy).

When ready to serve, place pieces of fish and shellfish in heated soup plates, and pour the liquid over. *Serves 6–8.*

ROMAINE AND ENDIVE SALAD

2 heads romaine, torn
1 head endive, torn
1 cup French dressing

Toss the romaine and endive with the French dressing. *Serves 8.*

PROFITEROLLES CHANTILLY

1½ cups heavy cream　　　　*¾ teaspoon vanilla*
4 tablespoons sifted　　　　*8 cream puff shells*
　confectioners' sugar

Whip the cream until stiff and fold in the sugar and vanilla. When the cream is ready you can add any of the following:

　1 teaspoon instant coffee
　¾ cup crushed peanut brittle
　¾ cup fresh fruit or berries
　¾ cup jam or ginger marmalade
　¾ cup toasted coconut
　1 tablespoon rum

Fill the cream puff shells. *Serves 8.*

Tahitian Bastille Day

Most Tahitians haven't the vaguest notion of what Bastille Day is all about, but the fact that it is reason for a celebration is quite enough for them. In Tahiti Bastille Day is simply called the Fête and is such a memorable event that in the islands the year is measured not from January to January, but from July to July. Unlike the more reserved French, who limit their celebration to a single day, the fun-loving Tahitians set aside at least two weeks for the occasion. We think that the Tahitians have the right idea and we're sure you will, too, if you inaugurate an annual fête of your own.

Loath as you may be to suggest costumes, in this case Tahitian-style clothes (sarongs, pareus, etc.) or casual sports clothes are the order of the day.

Cover your table with green burlap and make a centerpiece of tropical fruits and, if possible, hibiscus or other flowers. You'll find some wonderful Tahitian records available now and if anyone in your group has ever learned that incredible Tahitian dance, the tamure, there is no quicker way to break the ice than to get everyone out on the floor to give it a try. You'd be amazed how quickly even your most pompous friends drop their pretensions when trying to get their hips, legs and feet working in unison to the jackhammer rhythm of the tamure.

The menu for this Tahitian fête includes I'a Ota or Poisson Cru, an authentic Tahitian hors d'oeuvre as well as Chicken Momi and Kona Coffee Torte, which are not genuinely Tahitian, although their origins are in the Pacific. But authentic or not we think you'll find this feast so delicious that you'll start saving your pennies for the next flight to Polynesia.

I'A OTA or POISSON CRU

CHICKEN MOMI

RICE

TOSSED SALAD WITH MANDARIN ORANGES

KONA COFFEE TORTE

MAI TAIS or RUM PUNCH

I'A OTA

The Tahitians call it I'a Ota, the French call it Poisson Cru, and the Americans inaccurately call it Raw Fish. Whatever you call it, marinated fish is one of the treats of the Pacific.

It is impossible to give exact measurements for I'a Ota, for each time it is made creativity and imagination play a part in its preparation. However, Hugh Kelley, proprietor of the Bali Hai (a swinging hotel on the island of Mooréa, 12 miles from Tahiti) and an old hand at making I'a Ota, explained it this way to us.

"You'll need a good piece of fresh fish—either white sea bass, tuna or bonita—skinned and boned. Cut the fish into ½-inch chunks and place in a mixing bowl. Cover with well-salted cold water or sea water if you can get it and leave it for about half an hour. Drain the water off and add enough lime juice (reconstituted lime juice works best, since the Tahitian limes are much stronger than ours) to cover your hand when it is pressed on the surface of the fish. Allow the fish to marinate for about an hour, stirring occasionally. Drain and add one cup of coconut cream for every two cups of fish. You may also add chopped tomatoes, celery, onions and green peppers to taste. Be sure it's well chilled when you serve it and be sure to make plenty—everyone will be back for seconds."

CHICKEN MOMI

6 *boned chicken breasts*	*1 egg*
Salt and pepper	*1 tablespoon soy sauce*
2 slices white bread	*½ teaspoon ginger*
4 tablespoons half and half	*1 teaspoon salt*
1 small onion, minced	*2 tablespoons oil*
6 water chestnuts, sliced	*2 tablespoons honey*
¼ pound ground beef	*Sesame seeds*
¼ pound ground pork	

Pat the chicken breasts with a paper towel to dry, and sprinkle with salt and pepper. Soak the bread in the half and half and blend the mixture with the onions, water chestnuts, beef, pork, egg, soy sauce, ginger and salt. Place ⅙ of the stuffing on each piece of chicken. Tuck ends of chicken over stuffing and secure with toothpicks. Place in a baking dish and brush with oil. Bake at 325 degrees for 45 minutes or until meat is tender. Brush with honey and sprinkle with sesame seeds. Bake at 425 degrees for 10 minutes until tops are brown and crisp. Remove toothpicks before serving. *Serves 6.*

RICE

(See Index)

TOSSED SALAD WITH MANDARIN ORANGES

Salad greens
1 small can mandarin oranges
French dressing

Toss bite-size greens with chilled drained mandarin orange segments. Dress with your favorite French dressing.

KONA COFFEE TORTE

1½ tablespoons instant coffee	*3 teaspoons baking powder*
1 cup cold water	*¼ teaspoon salt*
6 egg yolks	*1 teaspoon vanilla*
2 cups sugar	*1 cup ground walnuts*
2 cups flour	*6 egg whites*

Dissolve the coffee in cold water. Beat the egg yolks until light and add the sugar gradually. Beat until thick. Sift together the flour, baking powder and salt. Gradually add sifted ingredients to egg mixture alternating with coffee. Add vanilla and walnuts. Beat the egg whites until stiff and fold into the batter. Pour into 3 buttered and floured 9-inch cake pans and bake for 30 minutes at 325 degrees.

ORANGE FILLING:

1 cup butter	*½ teaspoon instant coffee*
2 cups powdered sugar	*2 tablespoons cold water*
2 teaspoons cocoa	*2 tablespoons orange juice*

Cream the butter and add the sugar gradually. Add remaining

ingredients and beat until smooth. Fill the layers with this mixture.

FROSTING:

2 cups powdered sugar	*2 tablespoons cold water*
2 teaspoons cocoa	*2 tablespoons melted butter*
½ teaspoon instant coffee	*½ teaspoon vanilla*

Mix the sugar with the cocoa and coffee. Add the cold water, butter and vanilla. Beat until smooth and frost the top and sides of the torte. Garnish with walnut halves. *Serves 16.*

MAI TAIS or RUM PUNCH

You can buy either of these tropical drinks already prepared and your husband will be ever grateful to you for letting him out from behind the bar.

Fourth of July Watermelon Wallow

We read recently in one of those slick home and decorating magazines that Southampton's most gracious hostess is heralding the Fourth this year by sending out clever invitations, asking that the rest of the 400 "join them for fireworks on the lawn." Then afterward this same gay lady will serve a sit-down dinner for twenty-four in her old stable which she, in her off moments, has converted into a whimsical little dining gazebo. About all we can say to that is Phee-e-w.

Sadly enough, we'd have a pretty rocky time trying to emulate this patrician lady. Our lawns are plagued by our behemoth-like dogs, wayward divots and a virile stand of crabgrass. Even if we did have stables, chances are we'd be collecting social security before we got around to reaming out the last vestiges of the former tenants. And the mere thought of loping from kitchen to tackroom between each course sends us groping for the Miltown.

There's no need to wear yourself down to the ankles fixing up

Old Dobbin's abode to have an all-out Fourth of July melee. A Watermelon Wallow is the answer and a good relaxed form of mayhem that most everyone relishes in the heat of summer. Just think of those poor Southampton men all trussed up in their dinner clothes . . . and whoever heard of cavorting about the lawn with sparklers, tails flapping in the midsummer breeze?

Set the party mood long before the sound of the starting gun. With felt pen, write each invitation on an inflated balloon. Deflate and whisk into an envelope, along with a clean balloon. Your guests will have to blow one up to read it and then must letter their reply on the other and mail it back to you.

A good album of John Philip Sousa's mighty music should get things going in $\frac{4}{4}$ time, along with some strategically placed American flags. Set up a red, white and blue buffet table on the terrace and center it with a bouquet of sparklers for after-dinner revelry.

The whole idea of a Watermelon Wallow is that the lugs are placed at intervals around the lawn and your guests lie on their tummies, sipping convivially. When they tire of one group, all they need do is grab their straws and move on to greener melons. Let them go to work on the watermelons while you're tending to the rest of the meal. Supply them with red, white and blue beach towels to lie on and a fistful of straws and let them wallow.

LUGS

RUM PUNCH: (FOR 12)

1½ fifths Puerto Rican Rum	*1 sprig fresh mint*
1 pint lemon juice	*1 large jigger brandy*
½ pint orange juice	*1 large jigger gin*
½ pint orgeat syrup (from the liquor store)	*½ fifth dry white wine*

Watermelons

Mix lovingly. Pour over ice cubes and let stand for a few hours. Cut an oval scoop in the top of each melon and scoop out the innards. Taste the punch for any corrections.

Fill melons with the punch and 2–3 cups of the pulp. Chill, covered, for another 2–3 hours. One watermelon serves approximately 4 people, depending on how dedicated they are to wallowing.

When they start throwing the rinds, it's time to set up a buffet of

OLD GLORY SANDWICHES

FRENCH FRIES   STAR-SPANGLED SALAD

COFFEE CUMULOUS

OLD GLORY SANDWICHES

12 onion rolls, split and buttered
2½–3 cups sharp Cheddar cheese spread (the kind that comes in a crock is best)

3 cups chopped red onion
5 flank steaks
5 tablespoons Lawry's seasoned pepper

Heat the rolls 5–7 minutes. Smear about ¼ cup of cheese spread on the top half of the buns and sprinkle with ¼ cup of chopped red onion. Sprinkle the flank steaks with seasoned pepper and rub in with the heel of your palm. Throw them on the grill for about 2 minutes on each side for rare, 5 for medium rare. Slice thinly on the diagonal and place 5–6 slices on the bottom half of each bun. The meat will hang out of the bun considerably and if it really bothers you, you can trim it a bit. But after all that rum, who's going to care? Replace the top of bun to make 12 juicy sandwiches. (Plan on at least 2 for the men, maybe 1½ for the less genteel ladies.)

FRENCH FRIES

Take them out of the freezer if you can find your way after chopping all those onions. Heat according to directions.

STAR-SPANGLED SALAD

DRESSING:

¼ cup wine vinegar
½ teaspoon mustard
1 egg
2 green onions, diced large
2 hard-cooked eggs

1 bunch watercress
½ teaspoon salt
Dash coarse ground pepper
½ clove garlic
1½ cups olive oil

Iceberg lettuce, torn

Into the blender with all the dressing ingredients. Blend at high speed for 1 minute or until thick and smooth. *Makes 2 cups.* Serve tossed with iceberg lettuce.

COFFEE CUMULOUS

1 envelope gelatin (1 tablespoon)
¼ cup cold water
2 teaspoons instant coffee
½ cup water
4 eggs, separated

1 cup sugar
½ teaspoon salt
1 teaspoon vanilla
1 cup heavy cream
Semi-sweet chocolate

In a small cup, sprinkle gelatin over cold water to soften. In top of double boiler, dissolve instant coffee in ½ cup water. Beat yolks slightly and add to coffee. Add ½ cup of the sugar and salt. Cook over boiling water, stirring until thick and smooth. Remove from heat and add gelatin and vanilla. Cool. Beat egg whites until they hold soft shape, but are not stiff. Add remaining ½ cup sugar and beat until shiny and stiff. Beat cream only until it holds a soft shape. Pile on top of egg whites and fold the whole business into the coffee custard. Pour into a 2-quart soufflé dish. Chill 3 hours. Garnish with chocolate curls. *Serves 6.* (If you need more, it's easier on the nerves to make two separate recipes, rather than attempting to double. Egg whites and gelatin are temperamental partners and resent being mass-produced.)

To ensure that your friends will be around to celebrate the Fourth with you next year, bring on great urns of coffee with the soufflé and keep them hot while you're lighting the Roman candles.

Tomorrow morning your lawn's going to look as if Sherman himself had crossed on his march to the sea, but at least you won't have to clean the stable.

Cerebral Party

When you begin to suspect that dry rot has set in on your mind the time is ripe for a Cerebral Party. This may seem like a contradiction but, in fact, there is nothing like some stiff mental gymnastics to start your brain waves humming.

To get yourself into the mood dust off your dictionary and set about contriving a crossword puzzle, the answers to which form the invitation. Now that the party is a *fait accompli* and you can't back out, you'd better get busy. Gather up as many card tables as you can and cover them with black and white Op Art print vinyl (lovely stuff, no hems needed). Ferret out one of those large posters depicting the areas of the brain that doctors often display in their offices. Hang a print of Rodin's "Thinker" on your front door to set the mood.

As to the entertainment, all you have to do is provide the ingredients and your guests should be able to take it from there. Plan to have several types of activities going, so that your players can move from one table to another.

If you think that people might be slow to warm to the idea of the party, you might start out with a game that can be played by everyone before breaking up into smaller groups. Password or Twenty Questions are good choices, for nearly everyone knows the rules and can join in with some degree of enthusiasm. Don't be surprised, however, if you have some laggards. Some people have a passion for parlor games, while others look on them with the kind of loathing usually reserved for parsnips or the bubonic plague. However, once the evening gets rolling even these people will gladly join in as kibitzers and usually have as much fun as anyone.

After everyone is well into the activity of the evening you can set up the rest of the games. Chess, checkers, ESP, Scrabble, anagrams and Chinese checkers are all good options. Bridge takes too long and other card games don't have the proper intellectual aura for this party. For the non-players, set up one of those new round puzzles—one of the Op Art puzzles would be great here. This table may easily become the most popular as the evening progresses.

As for the food, plan a simple and informal buffet from which people can help themselves as hunger pangs strike. A hearty pea soup kept warm in a tureen, cold meats and cheeses and a selection of rolls should satisfy the body while the mind pursues higher goals. This also allows you to control the length of the evening by announcing dessert and coffee at the appropriate time. This is probably the only way to prevent having dedicated chess pundits still planning new strategies an hour before breakfast.

Prizes are always a problem, but for this party dictionaries, thesauruses or books of Double-Crostics are appropriate. Wine, too, is always a good choice and something everyone enjoys. The only real danger with this party is that your truly brilliant intellect will be revealed and public opinion will finally force you to accept that Fulbright grant you've been dodging.

SPLIT PEA SOUP
BASKETS OF BREAD AND ROLLS
MEAT AND CHEESE TRAY
WELL-BREAD PUDDING

IMPORTED BEER or A KEG
COFFEE

SPLIT PEA SOUP

"Beautiful soup so rich and green
Waiting in a hot tureen!"
LEWIS CARROLL

1 lb. bag split peas   *1 bay leaf*
Ham bone   *4 carrots, peeled*
1 onion, peeled and stuck with   *Water*
    2 cloves   *½ cup cream*
3 stalks celery

Soak the peas overnight in water. Place the ham bone, peeled onion with cloves, celery, bay leaf, peeled carrots and drained split peas in a large kettle. Add water to cover and bring to a boil. Lower the heat and simmer gently until the peas are soft and mushy (about 1½–2 hours). Pluck the ham bone from the kettle and puree the soup in an electric blender or mash through a sieve. Cut off any meat from the ham bone and sliver it. Pour the soup back into the kettle, add cream and taste for seasoning. Add ham and bring to a boil, but do not cook further. *Serves 6 and can be doubled or tripled for a large party.*

BASKETS OF BREAD AND ROLLS

Baskets of rye, whole grain wheat, French, European black and pumpernickel bread and rolls would be an opulent selection.

MEAT AND CHEESE TRAY

Spread a large tray with the likes of liverwurst, dry Genoa salami, head cheese, pepperoni, Swiss cheese, Gouda, Limburger and Cheddar.

WELL-BREAD PUDDING

10 slices bread
4 cups scalded milk
1 cup cream
4 eggs
1 cup sugar

1 teaspoon vanilla
1 teaspoon cinnamon
½ teaspoon nutmeg
½ cup melted butter
¾ cup seedless raisins

SAUCE:

3 egg yolks
1½ cups milk
1 teaspoon vanilla
1 cup sugar

1 tablespoon cornstarch
¼ cup water
1¼ ounces brandy

Break the bread into pieces. Combine the bread, milk and cream. Beat the eggs, toss in the sugar and mix until frothy. Add the bread-milk mixture, vanilla, cinnamon and nutmeg. Blend in the butter and raisins and pour into a greased 2-quart casserole. Set in a pan with about an inch of water in it. Bake at 350 degrees for 1 hour or until a knife poked in the middle comes out clean. To make sauce, beat the egg yolks in a saucepan and add the milk, vanilla and sugar, blending well. Cook over low heat until mixture bubbles. Combine the cornstarch with water and stir it into the milk mixture. Continue cooking until thick. Remove from the heat and stir in brandy. Cool and serve over pudding. *Serves 8.*

Wine Taster's Party

The grim and chilling specter of a pinched-nose sommelier has frightened away far too many of us from the delights of the grape. Too often you're left to stumble helplessly over a wine list while that sanctimonious authority stands tapping his pencil, heaving deep mournful sighs. But what wine *will* complement Beef Wellington, Filet of Sole Amandine and Chicken Curry, you wonder nervously. And when you finally do settle on something, the most you can hope for is a condescending nod before he whisks off to his sacrosanct domain, leaving you feeling artless and terribly, terribly gauche for having selected the Burgundy instead of an adequate little rosé.

Having witnessed any number of these painful scenes in the last few years (usually with our friends as the principal players) we decided the time had come to fight back. We began our clandestine educations one rainy Sunday afternoon when we gathered together a cellarful of willing and thirsty friends for a wine-tasting party.

We kept our guest list relatively small, for the memory of collegiate wine stomps where we drank cheap Paisano and came home with purple feet was still too fresh in our memories. Anything from 6–12 couples seems about right—but be sure not to include any of your acquaintances who consider themselves authorities. Even the most punctilious of guests can become posturing, sniffing, palate-cleansing charlatans when mingling with a flock of novitiates.

Since neither of us had authentic wine cellars secreted beneath our humble huts, we were forced to lean heavily on a few well-chosen props to transport us to the bosom of Epicurus. Judy managed to sweet-talk half a dozen barrels from a moving company and we covered each one with a red and white checked tablecloth. Leaving no cliché unturned, we finished off the tables with the candle-in-Chianti-bottle trick. Our invitations were dashed off with felt pens on red and white checked paper napkins.

While we waited for acceptances, we scrounged around for some French maps and were lucky enough to find one of the wine-producing regions. We made up a vintage chart to go with it (after having checked out enough wine books to scandalize the local librarian). Those same impressive books made a splash when distributed casually around the room. Be prepared to lose a bit of face though if your friends discover the library card lurking within.

We found that the wine dealer was happy to load us down with small booklets on wine that we also tucked about the room. Once in the wine shop we simply let the nice wine man hold our damp palms and help us make our choices. He told us that it's wise not to stray too far into the vines and attempt to serve too many varieties. It's more fun—and more informative—to restrict yourself in some way. You can select all red Burgundy wines and compare several different vineyards and vintages. Or compare two or three Burgundy reds with two or three red Bordeaux. Another interesting ploy is to test these against the New York and California comparables.

If you really want to put a damper on things, just start providing clean glasses for each new wine and wagging your finger at any guest who crassly drinks his wine instead of scrupulously rolling it about on his tongue. This is the kind of maneuver that has given the whole wine-tasting game its fearful reputation.

Occasionally life reverts to the blissfully simple. We found that the only accompaniment that wines need is a Vintner's Tray of cheeses, breads, fruits and a Fromage Glacé. We picked up an inexpensive wine rack at the liquor store and in each little cubbyhole tucked an individual setup of tulip-shaped wineglass, bright checked napkin and a fruit and cheese knife and fork. If your friends like contests you might even include a pad and pencil for ratings and offer small handbooks on wine or half bottles of good vintages as the prizes for those coming closest to the professional rating charts. Our own friends would have drummed us out of the corps had we tried this, since all of them think games like this are only slightly more hilarious than a college final. But you can sound out your own group for this kind of thing.

When everyone is settled with his first glass of wine, pass huge trays of husky wedges of cheese, crusty bread and iced fruit. If you feel shaky over selecting these Continental fruits of pleasure, here's some starch for your knees:

VINTNER'S TRAY

BREADS:

Thin sliced pumpernickel   *Unsalted soda crackers*
Sourdough French bread   *European black bread*

CHEESES: *Monterey Jack, Petit Suisse, Port du Salut, Bel Paese—choose whatever you like, but steer clear of the strong-flavored blue-veined cheeses this time, good as they are. They put up a nasty fight with the wine.*

FRUITS: *Apples, pears, peaches, thin slices of honeydew melon*

CONDIMENTS: *Sweet butter for those who like it and some small bowls of dry roasted almonds and sharp green olives.*

When we were recently in Dallas we found tucked away in Neiman-Marcus a warm and clever bon vivant so dashing that James Bond suffers by comparison. Mr. Victor reigns over Neiman's wine cellar and a more exciting kingdom can't be found. What you can find there is the coup de grâce for your party. You can't import Mr. Victor himself, but you can send for his LP record, *The Joy of Wine.*

As the crowning touch for your tasting party, bring in some fine champagne (Mumm's, Dom Perignon) and present your vainglorious Fromage Glacé surrounded by frosty purple muscats.

FROMAGE GLACÉ

½ cup whipping cream
½ stick butter, softened
1 tablespoon gelatin
¼ cup cold water
Hot water
1 ounce bleu cheese, crumbled

4 ounces Camembert, crumbled
2 ounces Liederkranz, crumbled
2 egg yolks, beaten until thick

Whip cream and set aside. Beat butter until fluffy and set aside. Soften gelatin in water and dissolve over hot water. Add cheeses to egg yolks and beat at high speed until creamy and smooth. Add gelatin and stir in butter. Blend thoroughly and fold in whipped cream. Pour into oiled mold and chill several hours. To unmold, dip in warm water to loosen and turn out on serving dish. *Serves 12 (small servings).*

Now what more can you ask for? With a loaf of bread, a jug of wine and your friends beside you, it's just got to be the best party this side of a vineyard.

Mexican Fiesta

Jack and Ken both have the sticky habit of issuing casual invitations to Christmas parties—without telling us. Usually the first clue comes when the Abbey Rents truck pulls up on December 20. And when the nice uniformed man asks for the lady of the house, it all becomes blindingly clear. They've done it again.

If the same bolt of lightning strikes you when you're not looking, pick yourself up from your ashen heap. Put on a wild Mexican fiesta—and one of the best times of all is Christmas when you can celebrate the traditional Fiesta de las Posadas. Without exception, your guests will fall upon otherwise pedestrian enchiladas with unwarranted alacrity. Remember they've been stoically suffering through the December gambit of Christmas party ham-and-turkey-on-the-sideboard, most often flanked by a shaky red thing that the hostess claims as her Christmas mold. Unfortunate, unloved and wholly accurate name. Mold, indeed.

While the Mexican people celebrate Posadas with a pageant each night for nine nights before Christmas, there's no need for you to conduct a marathon. Instead of the prescribed pageants and Christmas processions, you can make tree-trimming be your own form of Posadas. Trim the tree before dinner or afterward—whichever suits your plans best. Just remember that a gathering of well-oiled adults can often make a tree look like a love offering of a kindergarten crafts class, with tinsel and paper chains thrown at the tree with careless abandon. At any pass, make it a Mexican-spirited tree and supply paper flowers, papier-mâché ornaments and some of the more traditional Mexican straw and tin ornaments. If you're of a particularly artsy bent, you can make the paper flowers and papier-mâché yourself, thereby saving yourself the price of a face lift. If not, there are more and more avant garde boutiques springing up around the country, many of which carry all these items.

Boutique or Tijuana tourist trap—all can supply you with plenty of Mexican fired pottery for serving dishes and those amber-studded tin plates. Stock up on armloads of more floppy paper flowers for the house—and of course a Santa Claus piñata.

For a centerpiece distinctly Mexican, fill a sombrero with a bumper crop of red and green peppers and white onions. The combination not only looks Christmasy, but carries out the colors of the Mexican flag, also.

In Mexico, Christmastime is the time to light the Posadas candles. The Mexicans fill small brown paper bags about half full with sand or dirt. The top of the bag is rolled down once or twice for stability and a lighted candle rammed in the sand so that the flame is below the top level of the bag. The Mexicans line their streets with these glowing and inexpensive lanterns during Posadas, and it's an easy idea for your front walk or the corridor of your building if the super's understanding.

If you're bucks-up this Christmas, you can hire some strolling mariachis. If however your budget leaves you wondering what your mother-in-law is going to say when you serve hamburger patties and French fries for Christmas dinner, there's no reason not to let Herb Alpert and the Baja Marimba boys do the honors.

Hang the piñata out of sight somewhere until after dinner. And *qué bien comida* it is:

MARGARITAS
ALCACHOFAS CON OSTIONES
CASEROLA DE ENCHILADA RES
CHILES RELLENOS CON QUESO
ARROZ AMARILLO   TORTILLAS
CERVEZA
PIÑAS CON NATILLAS

CAFÉ   KAHLUA

MARGARITAS

True gourmets would frown on anything so strong before such a feast, but hang the taste buds. The Margaritas are good.

Lime rind   1 part Cointreau
Salt   1 part lime juice
3 parts Tequila   Crushed ice

Chill cocktail glasses, rub rims with lime rind and dip rim in salt. In a shaker, mix Tequila, Cointreau, lime juice and crushed ice. Stir; strain and pour into prepared glasses.

ALCACHOFAS CON OSTIONES
(Artichokes and Oysters)

3 large globe artichokes   Dash Worcestershire
3 dozen fresh or canned   Salt to taste
  oysters, chopped fine   2 tablespoons lemon juice
⅓ cup chopped little green   2 cups sour cream
  onions   Paprika
½ teaspoon Tabasco

Cook artichokes in simmering water for about 30 minutes. Remove, drain and chill for several hours. Arrange artichoke leaves on a serving plate and chop the hearts finely. Muddle the hearts, oysters, onions, seasonings and lemon juice until thick paste is made. Add sour cream and whip lightly until smooth. Place in bowl in center of leaves and sprinkle with paprika. (You can substitute 2 7-ounce cans of drained minced clams for the oysters if you like). *Serves 12 as an appetizer.* Or substitute Gazpacho (see Index) as a first course.

One of Mexico's traditional Christmas entrées is Mole en Guajalote (Turkey in Bittersweet Chocolate Sauce), which is enough to make any self-respecting gringo defect to Long Beach. We like this instead:

CASEROLA DE ENCHILADA RES
(Beef Enchilada Casserole)

2 *pounds ground round*	1 *quart tomato sauce*
3 *tablespoons oil*	½ *cup water*
3 *tablespoons chili powder*	2 *cups sliced pitted ripe olives*
1½ *teaspoons salt*	1½–2 *dozen corn tortillas,*
2 *teaspoons oregano*	*quartered*
2 *tablespoons paprika*	*Grated Cheddar cheese*
⅓ *cup flour (or less)*	*Chopped onion*

Brown ground round in oil and add chili powder, salt, oregano, paprika and flour (go easy; see how thick you like it). Stir well; add liquids and simmer for 10 minutes. Add olives, reserving a few, and simmer 2–3 more minutes. In a large greased pottery casserole that can weather both heat and cold, place layer of meat sauce and cover with quartered tortillas. Add approximately half of the remaining sauce and top with a really generous sprinkling of grated cheese and chopped onion. Cover with a layer of tortillas and remaining sauce. Lavish with chopped onion and grated cheese and a brave sprinkling of a few olive slices. (*) Bake at 350 degrees for 30 minutes or until bubbling and very hot. *Serves 12 generously.*

CHILES RELLENOS CON QUESO
(Cheese-Stuffed Chiles)

4 4-ounce cans peeled and   Flour
  roasted green chiles   8 eggs, separated
1 pound Monterey Jack cheese   ¼ cup flour
  (or brick, Muenster)   Vegetable oil

SAUCE:

2 medium onions, chopped   2 quarts chicken bouillon
¼ cup olive oil   Salt and pepper to taste
½ teaspoon garlic powder   2 teaspoons oregano
1 quart canned tomatoes with
  juice

Cut each chili into 2 strips and wrap each strip around a ¾-inch cube of cheese. Dip in flour. Beat whites and yolks of eggs separately. Fold yolks into whites and add ¼ cup of flour. Drop the chili-cheese contraptions into this batter and then into hot oil in frying pan. Baste with hot oil and when golden on one side, turn with slotted spoon. When golden on both sides, drain on paper towel. Either freeze at this point (*) or serve hot in a sauce of the remaining ingredients: Sauté onion in oil; add garlic powder. Add remaining ingredients and simmer gently for at least 20 minutes. Break tomatoes up slightly. This may be refrigerated and reheated to boiling at serving time. When ready to serve, drop the thawed chiles in the boiling sauce for 7–8 minutes or until puffed up again. *Serves 12 generously.*

ARROZ AMARILLO
(Yellow Rice)

2 cups regular rice, uncooked   1 quart plus 1 cup chicken
½ cup vegetable oil   bouillon
1 cup chopped onion   Salt and pepper

Heat rice in hot oil in large saucepan until just golden. Drain off excess oil and add remaining ingredients. Cover and simmer for 40 minutes or until rice is fluffy and no longer wet. *Serves 12.*

TORTILLAS
(Flat Corn-Cakes)

No need to grind your own corn on the back stoop. Smuggle some tortillas over the border or home from the supermarket. Heat and serve plain or with butter. Roll up and use as juice scoopers for the casserole.

CERVEZA
(Beer)

Dos Equis and Carta Blanca are both excellent brands of Mexican beer, available even in some parts of the East and Midwest.

PIÑAS CON NATILLAS
(Rum Pineapple with Custard Sauce)

4 large pineapples   *½ cup rum*
1 cup dark brown sugar *1 cup butter*

CUSTARD SAUCE:

6–8 egg yolks   *1 quart milk*
½ cup sugar   *2 teaspoons rum*
¼ teaspoon salt

Place pineapples on their sides on cutting board and slice off top third of each, leaving green leaves intact on the bottom two thirds. Cube the pineapple meat and lace with brown sugar and rum. Replace in pineapple shells, smear with bits of butter and cover with foil. (*) Slip into a 325 degree oven for 25 minutes. Remove foil and serve warm in the shells along with the sauce: Beat egg yolks and add sugar and salt. Scald the milk and stir into egg mixture very slowly. Place over boiling water in top half of double boiler and stir constantly until thickens. Put through strainer and cool. Add 2 teaspoons rum and chill thoroughly. This is a thin sauce; don't expect it to be firm. Makes 2 cups. *Serves 12.*

Retire to the den after dinner girded with coffee and Kahlua. There you can jab heartlessly at the piñata and amidst cries of Ándale and Fifty-four Forty or Fight, you'll probably elect Benito Juárez to succeed Dean Rusk. All this sounds like terribly bad form, but the combination of tequila, beer and Kahlua has a way of doing that. Award a bottle of tequila, tickets to a bullfight or a book on bullfighting to the one who manages to break the piñata and give each guest a lovely lighted candle to carry home.

As you pick Santy up off the floor (a mere shadow of his former self, poor dear) your man will cast a proud and gleaming eye upon you that's positively unruly. Olé!

The quick and the fed

8.

THE QUICK AND THE FED

For better or for worse. That's what the man said.

The "better" part conjures up different visions for each of us —for Jinx it's a weekend in San Francisco, for Judy it's lazy days on the beach. Maybe for you it's getting oodles of Valentines, all signed Guess Who. Or an unrumpled front page on the morning paper.

But we all knew what the parson meant when he said "worse." It's the late-dinner syndrome, of course. We're both chronic sufferers but even the most conscientious bride will experience the same symptoms now and then. You know the feeling—feverish brow, clammy hands upon the steering wheel as you speed through darkened streets knowing full well that your man came home to a cold and empty house half an hour ago. Most of us would rather sail the Trans-Pac in the teeth of a gale than go through this very often.

You think *you're* unhappy. Deliberate on how dispeptic he must feel. He can just about guess what's in store for him: a hastily composed duet of last night's tuna casserole with murmured apologies.

The thing is that there's really no need to apologize for drifting in with the sunset. Last-minute meals are an affliction that beset all of us once in a while. When you find yourself thundering in the door just ahead of your husband, you'll be kicking yourself for playing that last hand. But this is no time to be worrying about cause. Concentrate on effect.

Where effect is concerned all of us make an appalling strategic error. We scurry around the perimeter of the kitchen, heads down, hands fluttering tremulously from cupboard to mixing bowl and back again. Harried and haunted, we look more like victims of some exotic aberration than just dilatory chefs who stayed too long at the fair. This whole approach is wrong; all it does is beget a specimen case of nerves and assure our husbands that we've gone dotty at last. And still all we've done is reheat that tuna casserole.

First, an instant cook must hone her ESP to a keen edge. Prescience will tell you when it would be wise to use an hour in the morning to set the table, set up the coffee, put the meat out to thaw and formulate some sort of vague menu in your mind. If you don't, when the end is drawing near you'll stand tapping your foot while you peer with unseeing eyes at a can of salmon and a bag of stale potato chips.

If you *are* lucky enough to beat him home, Kismet is smiling kindly upon you. Get the car in the garage, but before you even strip off your gloves, turn on the oven and whisk out your pots and pans in legion. Even if he walks in the door at this moment, it looks better than nothing and he probably won't settle for the Athletic Club Thursday Night Buffet as a superior alternative.

Now, unless you're smack in the middle of a Saharan summer, light the fire and turn on the stereo. Or if it's at all plausible, take a note from Chapter 2, *Rekindling the Flame,* and set an intimate table for two in some different nook—on the patio, in the den, by the pool. Wriggle into a hostess gown or his favorite peignoir . . . that suit is a sure sign that you've been hobnobbing with the girls all day.

When you're an established last-minute cook, you find that the cocktail hour is of supreme importance. This is known in the trade as heading him off at the pass. Stir up some cocktails; have one yourself right now—just for pluck—and have his waiting for him when he comes in. Now's the time to bring out an hors d'oeuvre to fill in those first gaunt ravenings. And no matter if things are really in a state, be doing something terribly calm when he arrives. Pick up your creweling when you hear the key in the lock and smile benignly as he opens the door. Lovely.

Of course if you're caught, whey-faced, in the garage at 6:30 with your lizard pumps still on, you can't exactly say you're getting things ready for Goodwill. It's up to you to brazen it through as best you can. But if you're not discovered and dinner seems to be another soaring success, then by all means divulge your shameful little secret. He'll be doubly impressed.

Which brings us to the art of the alibi—something that habitual last-minute cooks master early in the game. It's entirely foolhardy to admit before dinner that you've been lingering at the furrier's or shooting a fast 18. Instead you must develop a line of do-good excuses that are totally irrefutable. Tell him you've been at the research library looking up the velocity tolerance of the new catamaran he's been wanting, or that you went to read to his invalid mother. How can he possibly argue with that? But like any wary criminal, make darn sure you're covered. Somewhere between the furrier and the links, you'd be smart to drop in on Mama.

That part's not so bad—we women have been adroit fibbers since Eve. But the next steps get a bit more technical.

Most of us are struck dumb by that inscrutable timer that resides so reprehensibly on the shiny panel above the oven. But a wise cook will take an already drab afternoon and curl up with the manufacturer's knotty instructions. Conquering the mystic world of this gadget gives you almost enough confidence to tackle a course in aerodynamics. You're free to plop a tidy Filet of Sole Veronique in the oven at 9 A.M., complacently certain that there'll be no slip-ups and that you've sloughed off the onus of the job.

Once you're over this technical trauma, the time comes to consider the aesthetic aspects. We learned long ago that a sprig of parsley and a scattering of slivered almonds goes a country mile in quelling our men's comments on what would otherwise be a plain old plate of lamb chops and string beans. To raise almost anything above the plebeian ranks, garnish it. Ice it. Flame it. But do *something* to it. And when it comes to recipes, beware of anything with umpteen steps. They're the things that slow you down far more than lots of required ingredients.

We've also discovered that "little" foods are aides-de-camp in our strategy. A roast is not only slightly ordinary no matter how succulent, but takes forever to cook. Thin slices of veal sautéed quickly in butter and drizzled with Marsala wine and chopped chives will go a lot farther for you. Briefly, the smaller, the better; little things just cook faster. And a tender cut of meat is much speedier—broiling and sautéeing take only a short 5–8 minutes, while braising and simmering are strictly for stay-at-home days when you planned to organize the bookshelves anyway. Perfect an elegant egg dish, cook your vegetables Chinese style—thinly sliced and crisp. Any fish or shellfish cooks in an instant and is terribly gourmet with just a splash of Chablis and a few mushrooms or some grated Parmesan. For that matter, learn that a hearty slosh of wine or sherry can make even yesterday's goulash smell aromatic and inviting.

But nothing will change the grate of his key to music without convenience foods. All this sounds expensive—wine, tender cuts of meat, shellfish, pre-packaged foods. And it is. But the tardy cook has long since acknowledged the brutal fact that the budget goes to the devil when dinner time rolls around. It takes cash to build up your cache, but every girl needs a luxury larder. Stock up on garnishes, packaged Noodles Romanoff, quick seasonings, canned seafood—whatever it is that your man craves. This way you can do your late-day planning not that afternoon, but days before in the aisles of the supermarket. In the warmth of spring, plant a few pots of fresh herbs so that if all else fails, you can still fill your kitchen with heavenly wafts of chives and rosemary.

Another important credo of the finish-line cook is that you need serve up only one glamorous dish. He'll be so busy being impressed with the intricacies of the Steak Diane (5 minutes, start to finish), he won't notice that the rest of the meal isn't in parade dress. Besides, a bona fide gourmet would blanch at the thought of absolutely everything being garnished and sauced. The simplicity of the other courses will merely serve as handmaiden to the elegance of your one perfect item.

While you're worrying over that single bit of manna, remember that there's one fatal trap. When pressed, it's our common failing to want to throw in everything but the kitchen sink and that, too, if there's room. What we all tend to forget is that one or two simple ingredients can blend to perfect harmony, while a whole bunch just seems sort of desperate. An old cup of coffee, vanilla ice cream and a handful of shaved chocolate all whipped together are marvelous. It's when you start lobbing on the whipped cream, maraschinos *and* pistachio nuts that you've destroyed its wee glimmer of hope. And never, never let it be known that it's only this morning's dregs, or you'll really jettison the bloom from the rose.

Now we could, in all legitimacy, present each of the forthcoming ideas as a shiny new recipe and even stoop to christening them with names like Shrimp Whiffle and Pink Dream. This would be fine and swell our book by another 20 pages or so, but even our flaccid consciences cringe at such chicanery. So what we'll do is merely hold up these ideas to pass in brief review for your militant inspection and then march ahead.

You'll notice that in lieu of giving each homely idea a proper name, we've put the main ingredient in mighty capital letters so that in your frenzy your glance will automatically come to a screeching halt at whatever it is you're seeking. We've also lumped them all together in their respective niches (appetizers, entrées, etc.) so that months from now (or tomorrow night if you're a perpetual dead-heat cook) when you have two tomatoes and no ideas beyond slicing them, you won't have to rack your already weary brain to remember if we had a recipe for Tomatoes Roly-Poly. Or was it Tomato Tempters? You can, instead, just riffle through to Vegetables, looking for TOMATO, and there you are. Still one giant step ahead of the family.

Appetizers, Soups, and Salads

When the dinner hour arrives only a few minutes behind you, you'll be feeling pretty secure if you know that you usually have a few cans of JELLIED CONSOMMÉ in the refrigerator. Then all you need do is wave almost any condiment over the consommé—

caviar, sour cream, chives, tiny canned shrimp, cracked black pepper or a lemon slice.

Augmenting your canned and frozen soups will increase your stature as a chef. Canned POTATO SOUP enhanced with cream and a substantial dash of sauterne should bring you a compliment or two. And dull old TOMATO SOUP rises above all others if you'll pitch in a diced fresh tomato and some frozen chopped chives or a pinch of chervil.

If there's a decided nip in the air, you may want to cultivate the Pepperidge Farmers. They've recently come out with the harried cook's dream—sumptuous CANNED GOURMET SOUPS, already seasoned to perfection and laced strongly with wine. All that's required is that you heat 1 can and serve to 2.

Or you can open a can of:

1. BEEF BOUILLON: Sauté onion slices in butter, add to bouillon and heat. Top with a slice of buttered French bread, a generous heap of Parmesan and slip under the broiler for a minute.

2. TOMATO SOUP: Sprinkle with chopped green pepper and serve hot in mugs.

3. TOMATO SOUP: Heat and scatter with crumbled bleu cheese and freshly chopped parsley.

For a cocktail hour appetizer:

1. BACON: Wrap slices around long thin soda crackers and broil until bacon is done.

2. SARDINES: Mash 1 can and blend with a little mustard, instant minced onion and softened butter. Serve with Melba toast and lemon wedges.

3. CHERRY TOMATOES: Use for dunking in guacamole.

4. CAVIAR: Spread on Melba toast. Sprinkle with lemon juice.

5. PICKLES: Halve a garlic pickle and hollow out ⅔ of the flesh. Stuff with cream cheese and cut in slices.

6. CELERY: Stuff celery stalks with deviled ham mixed with chopped green pepper.

7. Check Chapter 3, *Of Savages and Kings,* for more Eleventh Hour Appetizers.

Salads fill a big gap when there's a meager dinner in the offing. Almost any old thing in the refrigerator will dress up a salad:

1. Salami slivers
2. Capers
3. Chilled cooked asparagus
4. Cauliflower bits (raw or cooked)
5. Packaged croutons sizzled in garlic butter
6. Raw mushroom slices
7. Chilled canned beans (except baked!)
8. Raw zucchini slices
9. Crumbled bacon
10. Chopped hard-boiled egg
11. Leftover chicken, slivered
12. Chilled cooked beets
13. Canned water chestnuts
14. Raw bean sprouts

And a big Caesar salad will make a regular panegyrist out of him; the ingredients are all familiar staples and your behemoth cookbook has a recipe for it.

Entrées

No matter what else you do, the backbone of your dinner still remains the overwhelming question. It's fortunate that most men think a naked steak is solid gourmet fare, and this fact has saved all of us from sudden exposure at one time or another. But if your budget hasn't allowed for a 2-inch porterhouse or you didn't have time to swing into the Safeway, maybe some of the following will help:

1. CHICKEN LIVERS: Sauté in butter with chopped onions and pinches of one or two herbs he loves. Serve on toast.

2. STEAK: Cut a pocket in any tender steak and fill with canned oysters. Broil as usual and slice on the diagonal.

3. SCALLOPS: Sauté in butter, sherry and chervil. Garnish with slivered almonds. Good with stewed tomatoes.

4. LEFTOVER MEAT: Arrange a pretty platter of sliced cooked meat, sliced raw mushrooms, tomato wedges and artichoke hearts. Marinate and chill with a tart Italian or French dressing.

5. FISH: Top a halibut or swordfish steak with chopped green pepper, tomato sauce and grated Swiss or Jack cheese. Bake about 25 minutes at 350 degrees.

6. SHELLFISH: You can create a heavenly Newburg from a can of cream of shrimp soup, a dash of sherry and a can of shrimp or lobster. Serve in patty shells or over instant rice.

7. LOBSTER: Top broiled lobster tails with chopped macadamia nuts and a squirt of lime juice.

8. SPAGHETTI: To a package of reconstituted spaghetti sauce add some sautéed chicken livers and a dash of sherry and serve over cooked spaghetti.

9. EGGS: Spread toast with deviled ham from a can and top with poached eggs.

10. CREPES: Almost any leftovers will suffice when mixed with a cream sauce and rolled in crepes. Drizzle some cream sauce over the rolled crepes and broil for 1–2 minutes.

11. LEFTOVER MEAT: Looks pretty good to a hungry man when you doll it up with some wine gravy, mushrooms, onions and top it with refrigerator biscuits for a glamorous meat pie.

12. SHRIMP: Try Shrimp Sumatra (see Index).

13. LIVER: Try Lemony Liver for the Liver Lover (see Index).

14. GROUND ROUND: Make thin patties of seasoned ground round. Lay a slice of cheese and one of sweet onion on top of half of the patties. Sprinkle with crumbled bacon and press the second patty on top and seal edges. Pan-broil 3–5 minutes on each side.

15. LAMB CHOPS: Cut a pocket in large loin chops and fill with a tablespoon of crumbled bleu cheese. Close the incision with toothpicks and broil as usual.

16. FISH: Roll fish filets in melted butter, then ground almonds and sauté in butter. Serve with lemon wedges and tomato chutney or whatever you've got a lot of.

17. GROUND ROUND: Brown ground round with chopped onion, salt, pepper and chili powder. Throw in a dash of tomato sauce and simmer for a moment. Roll portion of meat mixture in tortillas that have been briefly fried. Cover it with more sauce and grated cheese and you have ENCHILADAS. Fry the tortillas a little crisper, tuck the meat sauce inside, top with shredded lettuce, grated cheese, chopped onion and tomato and you've got TACOS.

18. CANNED OYSTERS: Make a ceremony out of oyster stew. To canned potato soup add half-and-half, canned oysters, and giant slabs of butter. Heat in your chafing dish, lace with some warm brandy and flame right before his dazzled eyes.

19. FISH: As an accompaniment for cold poached salmon on a muggy summer day, stir up a tablespoon of mustard, a teaspoon of dill weed and ½ cup sour cream.

20. LEFTOVER CHICKEN OR TURKEY: Becomes a golden Divan when you place a few slices over cooked stalks of broccoli and top with a canned cream sauce. Sprinkle with Parmesan and bake for 12 minutes at 400 degrees.

21. FILET OF SOLE: Wraps easily around a few tiny canned shrimp. Secure with toothpicks and dump on a can of cream of shrimp soup. Bake 25 minutes at 325 degrees.

22. BEEF FILET: Try Fondue Bourguignonne (see Index).

23. STEAK: If you think of it in the morning, make a marinade of 1 can anchovy filets, mashed, 1 clove garlic, mashed, lots of cracked pepper, ½ cup olive oil and a smattering of chopped parsley. Marinate for as much time as you have, then grill, basting when you think of it.

24. GROUND ROUND: You can fashion a Hamburger Pizza by patting out 1½ pounds of ground meat in a circle about ¾ inch thick. Top with a can of tomato sauce, a sprinkling of mixed Italian herbs and throw on whatever you have hiding in the icebox. Top with some grated mild cheese and broil to desired doneness. Serve with cooked spaghetti that's been under the influence of some melted butter and your favorite herbs.

25. CORNED BEEF: Prepare biscuit mix and roll out in a large oblong about ¼ inch thick. Spread with mustard, top with slices of corned beef, sliced tomatoes and sliced Cheddar cheese. Bake at 425 degrees for 15 minutes. Cut in squares.

———

Now we have to renege and present 3 actual recipes, but they're all so easy that we won't even hedge about it. Alfredo made his reputation on fettucine and there's no reason why you can't follow the leader:

FETTUCINE

¼ cup melted butter
1 cup grated Romano cheese
½ cup heavy cream, whipped

1 8-ounce package egg noodles, cooked and drained

Mix butter, cheese and cream together and pour over cooked noodles. Mix slightly. *Serves 4.*

INCREDIBLE CRAB SOUFFLÉ

2 6-ounce cans white sauce
2 tablespoons mayonnaise
3 eggs, separated
1 can crabmeat

2 tablespoons grated Swiss cheese
Salt and pepper

Heat white sauce, stir in mayonnaise. Cool for a minute. Add egg yolks, along with crabmeat, cheese, salt and pepper to taste. Beat egg whites until stiff; fold into crab mixture. Bake in a souf-flé dish at 400 degrees for 25 minutes. *Serves 3.*

JAMBALAYA

This only *sounds* involved and is a savior if you have some left-over HAM.

4 onion slices	*½ teaspoon salt*
Dash garlic powder	*Healthy dash Tabasco*
½ green pepper, diced	*¼ teaspoon thyme*
2 tablespoons butter	*Pinch each basil, marjoram,*
1 small can solid pack toma-	*paprika*
toes	*1 cup diced ham*
¼ cup dry white wine	*½ cup uncooked instant rice*

Sauté onion, garlic and green pepper in butter. Add remaining ingredients (except rice) and bring to boil. Add rice and stir. Cover and simmer on low heat for 15 minutes or until rice is done. *Serves 4.*

Vegetables

It's almost axiomatic that when we're in a dither over dinner vegetables invariably take the rumble seat. But if the rest of the meal is so ragtag that it just can't be elevated, then vegetables it is.

Your first step is to invest in a set of skewers—those long lethal-looking things you'll find in the hardware store. On them you can impale any of the following:

1. ZUCCHINI slices/ CHERRY TOMATOES
2. Button MUSHROOMS/ tiny ONIONS
3. Chicken livers/ button MUSHROOMS
4. GREEN PEPPER chunks/ Pineapple chunks/ tiny ONIONS

5. Tiny ONIONS/ GREEN PEPPER/ CHERRY TOMATOES
6. ZUCCHINI SLICES/ Bacon bits/ GREEN PEPPER chunks

Brush any of the above with melted butter and broil.

In the realm of vegetables that you've just thawed and simmered for a moment, sometimes you're left with a pretty bleak presentation. Try topping them and slipping them into the oven for a second; you can use

1. Crumbled popcorn
2. Crumbled Fritos
3. Chopped nuts
4. Shredded Jack cheese
5. Toasted sesame seeds
6. Buttered bread crumbs mixed with Lawry's Seasoned Salt
7. Crumbled French-fried onion rings from a can

The rest of the grab bag includes:

1. TOMATOES: Open a can of tomatoes, add a dash of white wine, a pinch of oregano or basil and simmer 10 minutes.

2. ARTICHOKES: Cook, hollow out the choke and fill with heated canned Hollandaise sauce.

3. ZUCCHINI: Sauté slices of zucchini, add a can of tomatoes, half a cup of grated Parmesan. Heat to bubbling.

4. SPINACH: To a package of frozen chopped spinach add a pinch of instant minced onion and a glob of sour cream or crumbled bleu cheese. Heat through.

5. MUSHROOMS: Sauté in butter and fill with cooked frozen peas and tiny onions.

6. ONIONS: Top frozen onions in cream sauce with sliced natural almonds.

7. SPINACH: Cook frozen spinach and top with mixture of ground almonds, lemon juice and butter. Broil for a minute.

8. MUSHROOMS: Sauté caps and fill with mixture of ground almonds, parsley, butter and minced onion.

Side Dishes/Breads

If all you have secreted away in the refrigerator is a few lonely chops and an unfriendly package of frozen limas, harken back to your collegiate days when the house chef filled innumerable wide-open spaces with the likes of rolls, rice, potatoes and noodles. For starters, you can use:

1. RICE: Add a fistful of your favorite cheese to cooked instant rice and toss with parsley. Heat through.

2. BREAD: Heat bread sticks that have been dotted with butter and sprinkled with grated Romano.

3. ROLLS: Dip refrigerator rolls in melted butter, roll in sesame seeds, poppy seeds, caraway seeds. Bake according to directions.

4. ROLLS: Fill refrigerator crescent rolls with seeds, grated cheese, jelly, sautéed chopped onion or chutney. Roll up and bake as usual.

5. NOODLES: Toss cooked noodles with cottage cheese, cracked pepper and parsley or chives. Heat through.

6. NOODLES: Toss cooked noodles with a can of deviled ham, a little sautéed chopped onion and diced celery. Heat through.

7. POTATOES: Top baked potatoes with a glob of cottage cheese and sprinkle with paprika. Slip under the broiler for a moment.

8. BREAD: After you've fried hamburgers or pan-broiled a steak, cut thick slices of French bread and fry them in the drippings. Has sort of a Mason-Dixon aura, but men love it.

9. BREAD: Stir up a package of cornbread mix and throw in crumbled bacon, canned corn, cubed mild cheese, or chopped green chiles. Or any combination of same. Bake according to directions.

10. ROLLS: Prepare refrigerator biscuits, but pile one on top of the other and slip a wedge of cheese or what-have-you in between. Bake according to directions.

11. POTATOES: Roll frozen potato puffs in melted butter and bake as usual.

12. RICE: Toss cooked rice with grated Cheddar and cooked spinach. In and out of the oven in 10 minutes.

The nice thing about breads is that they thaw fast, and if you're thinking ahead, on some leisurely night you might try out a couple of ideas and stick them in the freezer. But then you probably won't. We never do.

Desserts

Considering the big picture, it's decidedly bad form to reserve your elegant dish for dessert, for by the time it arrives your man may be so mightily depressed over the meal that has preceded that nothing will lift him out of his blue funk. But if you're really up against it, try one of these:

1. BROWNIES: Add ½ package chocolate chips to a package of brownie mix. Top with the remaining chocolate bits and bake according to directions.

2. ANGEL FOOD CAKE: Fairly sings under the influence of cream whipped with a dash of instant coffee to the consistency of thick cake batter. Drizzle over toasted pieces of cake and sprinkle with shaved chocolate.

3. PUMPKIN PIE: Frozen pies are usually a dead giveaway but a frozen pumpkin pie isn't half bad when you top it with brown sugar and chopped pecans during the last 10 minutes of baking.

4. PARFAIT: Any old kind is always. impressive; try whipping softened cream cheese with a little confectioners' sugar and a dash of cinnamon and layering with any variety of berries.

5. PEARS: Mix a jar of currant jelly with a jar of light rum. Pour over chilled canned pears.

6. LEMON SHERBET: Drizzle light rum over scoops of lemon sherbet and call it Yo-Ho-Ho.

7. PARFAIT: Layer lime sherbet with a thawed package of frozen mixed fruits.

8. GINGERBREAD: Top with a dollop of sour cream and a preserved kumquat.

9. BANANAS: Bananas Foster has kept New Orleans going for years: Sauté halved bananas with brown sugar, butter, rum and if you have it, banana liqueur.

10. ICE CREAM: Whipped with almost anything is good—coffee, shaved chocolate, rum, Kahlua, nuts, your favorite liqueur.

11. FRUIT: Combined with sour cream and a garnish usually brings a smile. To any canned fruit, add a glob of sour cream and a dash of brown sugar, cinnamon, nutmeg, shaved chocolate, liqueur, or slivered almonds.

12. FRUIT: To two or more canned fruits add a stick of cinnamon and a jigger of rum. Heat and serve.

13. STALE COOKIES: Mash and soak with rum or liqueur and top with fruit, ice cream or just sour cream.

14. MANDARIN ORANGES: Chill canned segments until icy, top with a tablespoon of heated orange marmalade and a teaspoon of cold sour cream.

15. ORANGES: Soak fresh sliced oranges in orange curaçao and sprinkle with coconut.

16. SPICE CAKE: Prepare packaged mix and just before baking, top batter with sliced natural almonds.

17. APPLES: Sauté sliced apples in butter, brown sugar, cinnamon. Cover and simmer until fork-tender. Add ¼ cup currant jelly and simmer till jelly melts. Serve with a spoonful of sour cream.

18. MARRONS: Slice some canned marrons and add to a package of melted chocolate chips, along with a couple of tablespoons of the marron syrup and 1½ jiggers of rum. Serve warm over vanilla ice cream.

19. POUND CAKE: Toast slices of pound cake and smother with fudge sauce and slivered almonds.

20. POUND CAKE: Slice in four horizontal slices and smear melted chocolate between layers. Replace layers and chill.

––––––––––

If you're down to the absolute nitty-gritty, you can haul out the chafing dish and practice on some Continental COFFEE to ease his saturnine expression:

CAFÉ BRÛLOT

1 cinnamon stick	*4 lumps sugar*
3 whole cloves	*⅓ cup Cognac*
Slivers of orange rind (2 or 3)	*2 cups strong hot coffee*
Slivers of lemon rind (1 or 2)	

Warm first six ingredients in chafing dish. Ladle out a little of it, flame it and pour back into chafing dish. Stir until all's quiet; add coffee and when very hot, serve to two in demitasse cups.

CAFÉ OLÉ

2 tablespoons instant coffee	*2 cups water*
2 tablespoons chocolate chips	*Whipped cream*
2 tablespoons sugar	*Grated chocolate*

Combine all ingredients except last two in chafing dish and heat until chocolate is melted. Serve in teensy demitasse to two. Top with a little whipped cream and garnish with grated chocolate.

So the next time you're tarrying through the boutique, there's no need to break out in a rash when you glance at your watch. Dinner may be looming only a short hour away, but you have this smug set of helpmeets at home waiting for you and your man.

Our theory of relativity

9.

OUR THEORY OF RELATIVITY

No matter how long or how cleverly you manage to put it off, the wheel of fortune is bound to land on your number one of these holiday seasons and there you'll be with a lap full of relatives. If this is your first holiday *fête avec famille,* relax. Of course that's just what they tell sky-divers as they stand trembling on the brink of their first jump. And they get to pack their own parachutes.

Once you've made up your mind to take the plunge you must resign yourself to the fact that his relatives will automatically view you with a jaundiced eye, quickly deciding that he got the worst of the bargain. It's small comfort that your relatives are eyeing him with the same critical gaze. Just remember that once you have been drawn into the bosom of the family you'll be showered with recipes, advice and crocheted antimacassars. For that you can bide your time.

When preparing for an onslaught of the family be mindful that a houseful of mothers, fathers, aunts, uncles, grandmothers, nieces, nephews and cousins is a volatile mixture. If you are familiar with the whole tribe you're well ahead of the game. Just be sure to keep bearded Cousin Charlie, who goes to Berkeley and sports a Peace button, away from Aunt Minnie, who spies a Red under every bed.

Once you've got the adult factions in their respective corners you'll still have to do something to keep the kids from burning down your house out of sheer boredom. Forget sending them outside to play. When pushed, children develop an instant and deadly allergy to fresh air. So, once again, plan ahead. Set up some tables with games and puzzles and steer the kids firmly in their direction. If they don't seem to get the point, start one of the puzzles and they'll soon catch on. Be careful, though, not to get so wrapped up in finding the blue and purple piece with the square corner that you're drawn out of your concentration by the smell of incinerating turkey.

Another good way to keep the young set out of your eye shadow and racy paperback books is to put them to work. When Jinx was faced with her first family dinner she immediately marched out, stamp books in hand, and obtained an old-fashioned ice cream freezer. Churning kept a carload of kids out of trouble for a couple of hours. Remember, child labor laws are not in effect in the home. Let each child churn until he drops panting by the wayside and all you'll have to do is provide pillows for after-dinner naps.

CAVIAR CRAB COCKTAIL

OYSTER DRESSING   HERB-RICE DRESSING

THE MAGNIFICENT BIRD

GRAVY   WHOLE CRANBERRY SAUCE

PETIT POIS IN GLAZED ONIONS

MASHED POTATOES

BRANDY PUMPKIN PIE   STREUSEL APPLE MINCE PIE

BORDEAUX

The United States Navy, ever alert, has developed a computerized formula called Critical Path Analysis to ensure completion of a particular project on time. Though few of us have an IBM computer tucked in the breakfast nook, there's no reason why we can't adopt the methods of those savvy sailors for our own civilian purposes.

The Critical Path to Thanksgiving Dinner

Three days before dinner:
1. Begin to defrost turkey, if frozen
2. Make and freeze piecrusts

Day before dinner:

1. Make both turkey dressings, refrigerate
2. Finish making pies, cover with plastic wrap

Morning of dinner:

1. Set tables
2. Stuff turkey
3. Peel potatoes and place in water
4. Prepare onions
5. Place crabmeat in cocktail glasses, refrigerate
6. Set cranberry relish in dish, refrigerate

Six hours before dinner:

1. Begin roasting turkey

One hour before dinner:

1. Cook frozen peas
2. Place peas in onions ready for heating
3. Cook potatoes
4. Prepare cocktail sauce

One half hour before dinner:

1. Take turkey out of oven
2. Put peas in oven
3. Make gravy
4. Mash potatoes
5. Prepare crab cocktail
6. Make coffee

Just before sitting down to dinner:

1. Pop pies into the warm oven to heat for dessert

CAVIAR CRAB COCKTAIL

3 pounds fresh crabmeat
1 cup mayonnaise
1 cup sour cream
3 tablespoons lemon juice
3 small jars caviar

Divide crabmeat among 12 cocktail dishes. Make a sauce by combining all of the other ingredients and pour over the crab. *Serves 12.*

OYSTER DRESSING
(For the neck cavity)

½ cup celery, cut fine
½ cup margarine

1½ cups packaged dressing
  (unseasoned) or toasted
  torn bread
½ can oysters, minced

Sauté the celery in margarine. Add the dry dressing or bread and toss. The mixture should not be soggy but form a soft, loose ball. Add the oysters and toss again lightly. Don't pack this like cement into the innards or you will have a soggy, tasteless mess and it will serve you right. Use a gentle hand. *Makes 2¼ cups.*

HERB-RICE DRESSING

1 cup butter
1¾ cups chopped onion
3 cups diced celery, with leaves
3½ teaspoons salt
½ teaspoon pepper
2 teaspoons MSG

1¾ teaspoons sage
1 teaspoon rosemary
8 cups cold, cooked rice (about
  4 cups before cooking)
⅓ cup chopped parsley

Melt the butter over a low heat and add the onions and celery. When they are soft remove the skillet from the heat and add salt, pepper, MSG, sage and rosemary. Pour the butter mixture over the rice and parsley in a large bowl. Toss together and use to fill the body cavity of the turkey. *Makes 10 cups.*

DIRECTIONS FOR ROASTING TURKEY
(16–20 pound bird)

Preheat your oven to 325 degrees. Rinse the bird inside and out and gently pat him dry. Stuff the neck cavity loosely with the Oyster Dressing. Skewer the neck skin to the turkey's back and tuck the wing tips behind the shoulder joints. Rub the body cavity with salt and lemon juice before stuffing with the Herb-Rice Dressing. Shove the drumsticks under the little flap of skin at the tail or if your butcher has thoughtlessly nipped this off, tie them to the tail. Butter the skin thoroughly and sprinkle with lemon juice.

Place the turkey breast up on a rack in a shallow roasting pan. Cover with a loose peak of aluminum foil. When the turkey has cooked for about 4 hours remove the legs from the tail so heat can reach them. Continue roasting for another 2–2½ hours or until the drumstick moves up and down easily in its socket. Let the turkey stand 20 minutes before carving.

Apparently cooking turkey is one of the sacred womanly duties the younger generation never masters to the complete satisfaction of the older. When your mother (or, worse luck, his) pops out to the kitchen for a peek at the bird, just bide your time and ask for another glass of sherry. Your moment will come when the compliments are passed with the after-dinner coffee.

GRAVY

The making of good gravy is a mystery to us. Surely there is a foolproof way, but we tend to panic at the moment of truth and wind up with a bowl of lumps. If this is your problem too, now is the time to flatter your mother (or mother-in-law), hand her a pretty apron, your shameless adulation and ask her to do the honors.

PETIT POIS IN GLAZED ONIONS

12 Spanish or Bermuda onions	*2 10-ounce packages frozen*
Salt	*tiny peas*
Water	*Salt and pepper*
Butter	

Slice the top off each onion and cut out the center. Cook in lightly salted water until tender and drain. Put in shallow baking dish and pour melted butter over each. Cook frozen peas according to package directions. Season with salt and pepper. Fill onions with the peas (*) and heat in a 300 degree oven for 10 minutes. *Serves 12.*

MASHED POTATOES

12 medium-sized potatoes
2 cloves garlic
Salt
Water

1½ cups light cream
1 cube butter
Salt and pepper

Peel potatoes and cook with peeled garlic cloves in boiling salted water until tender. Drain and shake over the heat to dry. Discard the garlic and mash the potatoes, adding the light cream, butter and salt and pepper to taste. *Serves 12.*

BRANDY PUMPKIN PIE

1¾ cups pumpkin
1 cup sugar
1½ cups evaporated milk
¼ cup brandy
3 teaspoons pumpkin pie spice

1 large egg, slightly beaten
½ teaspoon salt
9-inch piecrust
Whipped cream
Powdered sugar

Mix together all ingredients except crust, cream and sugar. Pour into chilled piecrust and bake at 425 degrees for 15 minutes. Turn the oven down and cook at 350 degrees for 35 minutes or until the filling is set on the outside and fairly firm in the middle. Chill and serve with cream that has been whipped with powdered sugar. *Serves 12.*

STREUSEL APPLE MINCE PIE

Unbaked 9-inch pie shell
2 cups mincemeat
3 cups sliced, peeled apples
⅓ cup sugar

1 tablespoon lemon juice
½ cup sugar
½ cup flour
¼ cup butter or margarine

Line the pie shell with mincemeat. Mix apples and ⅓ cup sugar and the lemon juice. Place the apples on top of the mincemeat. Mix ½ cup sugar and flour. Blend in butter and sprinkle over the apples, covering well. Bake in a 450 degree oven for 10 minutes. Reduce heat to 325 degrees and bake for 45 minutes longer.

Serves 6.

When the big day is over the hostess is left with the thankless task of dealing with that hulking carcass. Of course there is the endless procession of hot turkey sandwiches and cold turkey sandwiches. But if that's where your imagination or patience ends try one of these. If you're lucky your husband may not even realize that it's just the same old turkey that for days has stared at him sullenly each time he's opened the refrigerator door.

TIJUANA TURKEY

1 package tortillas
4 thick slices turkey
1 chopped onion
1 or 2 cans (4 ounce) green chili salsa

Cheddar cheese, grated
1 can cream of chicken soup
1 can mushroom soup
1 cup milk

Butter a casserole dish and place in the bottom 4 tortillas cut in quarters. Cover with 2 slices turkey cut in small pieces, onion, chili sauce and grated cheese. Add a layer of the 2 cans of soup mixed well with milk. Repeat another layer of all the ingredients and finish with the tortillas. Place in the refrigerator for 24 hours. (*) Bake at 300 degrees for 1½ hours. *Serves 4.*

TURKEY PAELLA

1 1-pound-12-ounce can tomatoes
½ cup water
¼ cup olive oil
¼ cup chopped onion
¼ cup chopped green pepper
1 teaspoon salt
1 teaspoon garlic salt

Dash cayenne
¾ cup long-grain rice
1 package frozen artichoke hearts, thawed and quartered
1½ cups diced cooked turkey
¼ cup sliced stuffed green olives

Combine tomatoes, water, oil, onion, green pepper and seasonings in a large saucepan. Add rice and artichoke hearts; cover and bring to a boil. Reduce the heat and simmer, covered, for about 20 minutes or until the rice is tender. Stir in turkey and olives. Heat until boiling and serve. *Serves 4.*

TURKEY AND HAM SHAZAM

(So good it would make Mary Marvel)

2 boxes frozen broccoli—	½ teaspoon salt
cooked and drained	Pepper
¼ cup melted butter	½ cup Parmesan cheese
¼ cup flour	6 slices turkey
2 cups chicken broth	6 slices ham
½ cup heavy cream	½ cup sliced mushrooms
3 tablespoons sherry	

Place broccoli in a casserole dish crosswise with stems in. Place melted butter in a saucepan. Add flour to make a paste. Stir in chicken broth, cream, sherry and salt and pepper. Stir until thickened. Pour half of the sauce over the broccoli and add Parmesan to the rest. Arrange turkey and ham slices over the broccoli and top with mushroom slices. Pour the cheese sauce over all (*) and bake in a 350 degree oven for 20 minutes. Place under the broiler for a couple of minutes to brown. *Serves 4.*

Christmas often brings, along with good cheer, a house full of guests. Although few new houses are equipped with guest rooms, most families past the apartment-with-pull-down-bed stage can make some provision for overnight visitors if it is only a pillow and army blanket tossed unceremoniously on the living room couch.

There's certainly nothing wrong with that for nieces and nephews and an occasional visiting fireman, but if you're considering bedding down your in-laws in this cavalier manner, you'd do better to suggest the nearest motel.

On the other hand, if you do have a guest room or other reasonably adequate facilities for family transients there are a few precautions you can take to ensure that their stay with you will receive rave notices.

First there's the bed. If your guest room bed resembles a trembling mass of tapioca, don't even consider having anyone spend so much as a night with you until you can beg, borrow or steal a good firm mattress. Be sure that you have plenty of blankets on the bed or within easy reach. No quantity of hot breakfast coffee will warm the good humor of a frostbitten in-law.

Speaking of coffee, why not put a thermos of it and a couple of cups in the guest room for the benefit of early risers. While you're at it, check to see that you have provided good reading lights, ashtrays, cigarettes, a clock with an alarm and a couple of good books. Collections of short stories or essays are great since, unlike an unfinished novel, they can be left behind without regret. Don't forget cleansing tissue, a couple of new toothbrushes in case of emergency and a flashlight—even big cities are the helpless victims of the likes of Con Edison. Some gracious additions to the guest room are stationery, note pad and pencils, stamps, a sewing kit and some sachet in the drawers. A welcoming bouquet of flowers adds the finishing touch.

Now that the guest room is up to a white-glove inspection by the most fastidious relative, the time has come to get back to their gastronomical welfare.

Christmas Eve Supper

OYSTER STEW
SALAD MIMOSA
LINDA'S HERB PINWHEEL LOAF
CHRISTMAS COOKIES

CHABLIS or BEER

OYSTER STEW

8 cans frozen oyster stew   ¾ cup dry sherry
8 cans half and half   Butter
1 pint oysters

Heat the frozen stew and add 8 stew cans of half and half and simmer over a low heat. Stir in the oysters and simmer for 5 minutes longer. Add sherry. Pour into heated soup plates and serve with a chunk of butter floating on top. *Serves 16.*

SALAD MIMOSA

¾ cup olive oil   1 clove garlic, finely minced
3 tablespoons wine vinegar   5 quarts crisp salad greens
1½ teaspoons salt   5 hard-cooked eggs, finely
¼ teaspoon cracked pepper   chopped

Combine the oil, vinegar, salt, pepper and garlic in a jar. Shake well. Place the greens in a salad bowl; add the dressing and toss vigorously. Sprinkle with chopped egg. *Serves 12.*

LINDA'S HERB PINWHEEL LOAF

1 package hot-roll mix
2 eggs
2 tablespoons grated Parmesan cheese
½ cup chopped parsley

2 tablespoons chopped chives
½ teaspoon onion salt
2 tablespoons butter or margarine

Prepare the hot-roll mix, including 1 egg, and let rise. Beat the other egg and stir in the cheese. Heat the remaining ingredients until the herbs are just wilted. Cool and blend in beaten egg-cheese mixture. Punch the risen dough down and knead a few times. Roll out to a rectangle. Spread with parsley-chive mixture and roll up like a jelly roll. Place with the seam side down on a greased cookie sheet. Cover with a cloth and let rise until double in bulk (about 45 minutes). Bake in a 375 degree oven for 45 minutes or until the bread gives a hollow sound when tapped. Remove from the pan and cool. *Serves 16.*

CHRISTMAS COOKIES

Certainly you have at least one friend who greets the Yuletide season with a kitchen marathon. She probably makes minuscule gingerbread men for the children in the neighborhood and regales her friends with Rum Balls, Marzipan, cookies of all description, and fruit cake in old coffee cans. She may be a perfectly sensible girl at any other time of the year, but at Christmas she reads too many women's magazines.

But from your point of view she is a blessing in disguise, for her bundles of goodies will save you hours of dessert-making. So watch your neighbor with indulgent interest, lend her a cup of sugar if she needs it, but never, never read anything but fashion magazines during the Christmas season or you may find yourself putting chocolate eyes on 7 dozen gingerbread men.

Christmas Breakfast

CRANBERRY AND ORANGE JUICE WITH MINT
BAKED BACON AND SAUSAGE
SCRAMBLED EGGS   EGGNOG WAFFLES
COFFEE

CRANBERRY AND ORANGE JUICE WITH MINT

Mix 1 quart orange juice and 1 quart cranberry juice. Pour into iced glasses and garnish with mint sprigs. *Serves 8.*

BAKED BACON AND SAUSAGE

Arrange 16 slices of bacon and 16 link sausages on broiler pans or on wire racks placed in shallow pans. Bake in a hot oven (400 degrees) for about 15 minutes until nicely browned. Drain off drippings as the meat cooks. *Serves 8.*

SCRAMBLED EGGS

1 dozen eggs
Salt and pepper
2 tablespoons butter

3 heaping tablespoons sour cream
Chopped chives

Beat eggs until frothy and add salt and pepper. Pour into a pan coated with melted butter. Add the sour cream after the eggs have begun to set. Continue cooking just long enough to set; sprinkle with chives and serve. *Serves 8.*

EGGNOG WAFFLES

1⅓ cups buttermilk
⅔ cup commercial eggnog
2 eggs, slightly beaten
2 tablespoons oil

½ teaspoon soda
¼ teaspoon nutmeg
2 cups prepared pancake mix
½ cup chopped walnuts

Blend together the buttermilk, eggnog, eggs, oil, soda and nutmeg. Add the pancake mix and the chopped walnuts. Mix again. Bake in a hot waffle iron. *Serves 8.*

Christmas Dinner

CHICKEN AND TURTLE SOUP
ROAST GOOSE WTH APPLE DRESSING
GLAZED MASHED POTATO RING
CARROTS IN DILLED WINE SAUCE   GREEN BEANS
HOT ROLLS
PLUM PUDDING   HARD SAUCE
CHÂTEAUNEUF DU PAPE

CHICKEN AND TURTLE SOUP

3 cups clear chicken broth
2 (1 pound 4 ounce) cans
   clear turtle soup

½ cup dry sherry
8 slices lemon

Combine broth and turtle soup. Add sherry and bring to a boil. Serve hot with a slice of lemon topping each serving. *Serves 8.*

ROAST GOOSE WITH APPLE DRESSING

6 large tart apples	3 tablespoons sugar
½ cup butter	1 teaspoon salt
1 cup diced celery	1 teaspoon nutmeg
2 cups toast crumbs	1 8-pound goose
¼ cup melted butter	

Core and dice the apples and sauté them in the ½ cup butter. Add celery and cook until crisp but tender. Combine with toast crumbs that have been mixed with ¼ cup melted butter. Add sugar, salt and nutmeg.

Stuff the goose lightly with this mixture and close opening by sewing or lacing and put on a rack in an open pan. Place in a preheated 400 degree oven and immediately reduce heat to 325 degrees. Roast for 2½–3 hours. Prick the skin occasionally to drain off fat. Serve on a platter surrounded by spiced crab apples. *Serves 8.*

GLAZED MASHED POTATO RING

1 cup grated sharp Cheddar cheese
6 cups mashed potatoes
2 tablespoons melted butter

Stir cheese into the mashed potatoes until well blended. Turn into a greased 2-quart ring mold. Brush the top with a tablespoon of melted butter. Bake in a 400 degree oven for 25 minutes or until the top is golden. Unmold the ring onto a heatproof serving platter. Brush the top with the remaining tablespoon of butter and run under the broiler for 3–5 minutes. Garnish with watercress. *Serves 8.*

CARROTS IN DILLED WINE SAUCE

3 tablespoons butter	1½ tablespoons cornstarch
¾ teaspoon dill	½ teaspoon garlic salt
¾ cup white wine	Drop of Tabasco
2 tablespoons minced onion	1½ tablespoons lemon juice
¾ cup chicken broth	4 cups hot cooked sliced carrots

Melt the butter in a saucepan and add dill, wine and onion.

Combine broth with the cornstarch and add to the contents of the saucepan. Toss in the salt, Tabasco and lemon juice. Cook, stirring over a moderate heat until the sauce thickens. Add carrots and lower heat. Simmer gently for 5–10 minutes. *Serves 8.*

GREEN BEANS

2 packages frozen green beans
2 tablespoons butter
Salt and pepper

Cook the beans according to the package directions, but cheat a bit on the cooking time they suggest. Vegetables should be slightly crisp, not limp and haggard when they come to the table. Top with butter, season with salt and pepper. *Serves 8.*

PLUM PUDDING

This pudding, a plump beauty, is straight out of Dickens and should be carried majestically to the table borne on a heady sea of flaming brandy.

3 cups dried white bread
crumbs
½ teaspoon salt
¾ teaspoon ground nutmeg
¼ teaspoon cloves
½ teaspoon cinnamon
½ cup scalded milk
¼ cup sherry
1 cup suet
½ cup granulated sugar
¼ cup brown sugar
¾ cup chopped raisins

¾ cup whole raisins
½ cup currants
¼ cup citron
¼ cup candied lemon peel
¼ cup candied orange peel
¼ cup dates, chopped
½ cup tart apples, chopped
¼ cup slivered almonds
¼ cup brandy
6 eggs, well beaten
½ cup brandy

After you have assembled all the ingredients you'd better take a whiff of smelling salts—you're probably feeling slightly faint. When you have recovered, mix the bread crumbs with the spices and soak in scalded milk and sherry for 2 hours. Chop the suet and mix with your hands until it is creamy. Add the soaked bread, the sugar, the fruit and the nuts. Mix well with the ¼ cup brandy and eggs until the fruit and nuts are evenly distributed. Place in a greased 2-quart mold. Seal the top securely with foil and place in the bottom of a kettle. Add enough boiling water to half cover the mold. Cover the kettle and steam over a low heat for 5–6 hours. Check the kettle periodically to see if more water is needed. When ready to serve, unmold onto a platter, warm ½ cup brandy and pour over the pudding. Set it aflame (be careful in this operation, Jinx walked around without eyebrows for months after her first try at flambé) and carry it into the darkened dining room to watch your guests' eyes match the glow.

If you like a sauce with your plum pudding here is a simple and delicious one.

HARD SAUCE

½ pound butter
1½ cups powdered sugar
4 tablespoons rum or Cognac

Cream the butter and then beat in the sugar and liquor. Keep chilled until serving time. *Serves 8.*

Your Christmas dinner guest list will undoubtedly include a few children. You will find that members of the younger set will turn up their charming pug noses at such exotic fare as Glazed Mashed Potato Ring, Carrots in Dilled Wine Sauce or Plum Pudding. To stave off the slight gagging sounds that would otherwise punctuate the dinner table conversation, be sure to set aside some plain mashed potatoes and carrots, as well as a quart or two of vanilla ice cream.

————

When the tulips begin to pop up from the window box and your husband starts studying the baseball schedule you'll know it's spring and time to begin thinking about . . .

Easter Dinner

CHILLED SPINACH SOUP
HAM EN CROUTE
ASPARAGUS PARMESAN
ENORMOUS POPOVERS
CREAM CHEESE AND STRAWBERRIES
ANJOU ROSÉ

CHILLED SPINACH SOUP

*1 large package frozen chopped
 spinach*
*3½ cups spinach liquid and
 milk*
3 tablespoons butter
*½ teaspoon instant minced
 onion*
*2 tablespoons finely diced
 celery*

3 tablespoons flour
¾ teaspoon salt
Pinch pepper
*½ cup light cream (or half and
 half)*
1 chicken bouillon cube

Cook spinach according to the directions on the package. Drain
and reserve the liquid. Add milk to the spinach liquid to make
3½ cups. Melt butter and add onion and celery. Sauté for 1 minute and stir in flour, salt and pepper. Add milk mixture and cream
gradually. Add bouillon cube and cook over very low heat until
thickened. Add spinach and blend. Chill thoroughly and put
through a blender just before serving. *Serves 6.*

HAM EN CROUTE

1 teaspoon powdered thyme	½ cup ice water or boiling
½ teaspoon powdered rosemary	water
¼ teaspoon salt	1 5-pound canned ham or fresh
¼ teaspoon pepper	ham cooked to your taste
2 packages piecrust mix	1 egg yolk
	1 tablespoon milk

Add the thyme, rosemary, salt and pepper to the piecrust mix. Add water (check the package directions to find out whether to use boiling or ice water—they can't seem to get together on this) and toss lightly. When the pastry forms a soft ball roll it out to a ½ inch thickness. Place the ham in the center and wrap it in the pastry. Moisten the edges of the pastry, join them and seal tightly. Roll out leftover pastry and cut into leaf shapes. Moisten the pastry leaves and place on the ham's slipcover. Beat egg yolk with milk and brush over pastry. Bake at 350 degrees for 45 minutes until the crust is golden. *Serves 6 with leftovers.*

ASPARAGUS PARMESAN

2 pounds fresh asparagus	½ cube butter, melted
Salt and pepper	½ cup grated Parmesan cheese

Cut off the tough stalk ends of the asparagus and arrange the stalks in a skillet. Cover with salted water and cook until tender but crisp (about 4–6 minutes). Drain and dress with salt, pepper and butter. Sprinkle with Parmesan cheese. *Serves 6.*

ENORMOUS POPOVERS

4 teaspoons shortening	1 cup milk
1 cup sifted flour	2 eggs
½ teaspoon salt	

Heat oven to 425 degrees. Put shortening in bottom of 7–8 custard cups which have already been greased. Put cups on a cookie sheet and put in the oven for 5–10 minutes. Sift dry ingredients into a bowl, add wet ingredients and beat with a rotary beater *just until smooth.* Pour into custard cups (about ½ full) and bake at 425 degrees for 30–45 minutes depending on the eccentricities of your oven. *Makes 7–8 popovers.*

CREAM CHEESE AND STRAWBERRIES

1 cup whipped cottage cheese   *½ teaspoon vanilla*
1½ cups sour cream   *3 boxes fresh strawberries*
1 cup confectioners' sugar

If you can't find already whipped cottage cheese, beat regular cottage cheese until smooth. Add sour cream, sugar and vanilla. Beat again and pour cheese mixture into 8 muffin-size paper liners. Put in muffin pan cups and freeze until firm—about 2 hours.

When ready to serve remove the cheese from the paper liners and turn onto serving dishes. Let stand for 15 minutes at room temperature to soften. Serve with hulled fresh strawberries.

Serves 8.

Just because the major holidays have been taken care of don't think for a moment that you're secure. Relatives, like summer thunderstorms, often appear out of a clear blue sky.

This menu is a sneak attack on those visiting relatives who regard cooking with spirits as the first step to *The Days of Wine and Roses* and look upon the use of garlic as an exotic and foreign affectation. They will be blissfully content with this chintz and milk-glass dinner. And about the cup of wine and the 5 cloves of garlic—if anyone should ask what makes the meat taste so good just zip your lip and pass the after-dinner mints.

UNDERCOVER POT ROAST
EGG NOODLES
ZIPPY ZUCCHINI
PEAR AND CHEESE CRISP WITH VANILLA ICE CREAM

UNDERCOVER POT ROAST

4 tablespoons olive oil	*2 onions, halved*
1 brisket of beef or chuck roast	*3 sprigs of parsley*
1 cup dry white wine	*2 bay leaves*
2 cups canned tomatoes	*Salt and pepper*
5 small cloves of garlic, put through a garlic press	*1 tablespoon Italian seasoning*

Heat the olive oil in your largest, heaviest-bottomed pot. Brown the chunk of meat well on all sides and pour in the wine. Turn down the heat and add the tomatoes, garlic, onion, parsley, bay leaves and salt and pepper to taste. Toss in the seasonings and cover. Simmer for 4 hours, turning the roast once. Remove to a warm platter. Skim the fat from the gravy and serve over a mountain of golden egg noodles. *Serves 6.*

ZIPPY ZUCCHINI

1 cup walnut halves	*2 tablespoons butter*
6 medium zucchini	*Salt and pepper*

Save enough walnuts to use for garnish and chop the rest. Cut unpeeled zucchini in slender slices. Sauté in butter, stirring constantly. When the zucchini is nearly done, add the nuts and salt and pepper. Continue cooking until just tender. Garnish with walnut halves. *Serves 6.*

PEAR AND CHEESE CRISP

3 large pears	*½ teaspoon ground ginger*
1 tablespoon lemon juice	*1 cup grated sharp Cheddar cheese*
¼ cup granulated sugar	

TOPPING:

½ cup light brown sugar, firmly packed	*Dash salt*
¼ cup sifted flour	*¼ cup butter*

Halve, core and slice the pears. Place them in a greased baking dish. Sprinkle with lemon juice. Combine sugar, ginger and cheese; sprinkle over pears and set aside. (*) Combine brown sugar, flour and salt in a bowl. Cut in butter with a pastry blender or 2 knives until the mixture resembles coarse oatmeal. Sprinkle evenly over the pears. Bake, uncovered, in a 350 degree oven for 45 minutes or until the pears are tender and the topping golden. Serve warm with vanilla ice cream. *Serves 6.*

Here is a menu to please that suave bachelor uncle of yours or your husband's aunt who wears hats to the office and neatly polishes off 3 martinis before dinner.

CREAM OF CRESS SOUP
CHIC CHICKEN
TOMATO ASPIC
FRENCH BREAD
DAIQUIRI TORTE

GRAVES WHITE WINE

CREAM OF CRESS SOUP

½ cup chopped onion
2 tablespoons butter
1 tablespoon flour
2 cups milk
1 bunch watercress, chopped

1 teaspoon celery salt
1½ teaspoons salt
1½ cups half and half
½ cup heavy cream

Sauté onion in butter until blond. Stir in flour, making a smooth paste. Add milk and continue stirring. Add chopped watercress, celery salt and salt. Simmer gently for 10 minutes. Add half and half and heavy cream. Add more salt if necessary. *Serves 4 generously.*

CHIC CHICKEN

1 frying chicken (about 3
    pounds) cut in pieces
3 tablespoons olive oil
1 small onion, minced
½ pound fresh mushrooms
4 slices prosciutto

2 bay leaves
⅛ teaspoon powdered thyme
3 sprigs parsley, minced
Salt and pepper
1 cup white wine
1 cup consommé

Wash and dry the chicken pieces and brown on all sides in the hot olive oil. Remove the chicken and add onion to the pan. Wash and slice the fresh mushrooms and add to the pan. Brown the mushrooms and onion lightly. Put chicken back in the skillet with the rest of the ingredients. Bring to a boil, cover and turn down heat to a simmer. Cook for 30 minutes or until chicken is tender and the sauce is reduced. *Serves 4.*

TOMATO ASPIC

1 package celery-flavor gelatin
1 cup tomato juice or mixed
    vegetable juice
¾ cup chilled tomato juice or
    mixed vegetable juice
2 tablespoons vinegar
2 tablespoons lemon juice

¼ teaspoon paprika
½ cup celery, diced
½ cup green pepper, diced
½ cup minced onion, diced
Watercress
Sliced lemon

Dissolve the gelatin in 1 cup of the tomato juice and heat until boiling. Cool and combine with the ¾ cup chilled tomato juice, vinegar and lemon juice. Chill until slightly thickened and add the paprika and diced vegetables. Pour into a 1-quart mold and chill at least 3 hours or until firm. Unmold and garnish with watercress and lemon slices.

DAIQUIRI TORTE

CRUST:

½ *cup flour*
2 *tablespoons sugar*
½ *stick butter or margarine*

FILLING:

2 *eggs*
½ *cup water*
1 *teaspoon rum extract*
⅔ *cup sugar*
1 *envelope (1 tablespoon) un-*
flavored gelatin

1 *6-ounce can frozen daiquiri*
mix
1 *cup whipping cream, whipped*
Grated lime rind

Combine the crust ingredients and press firmly into the bottom of a 9-inch spring form pan or a 9×9-inch greased baking pan. Bake in a 350 degree oven for 10 minutes. Cool.

To make the filling, break the eggs into the top of a double boiler and beat slightly. Add the water, rum extract, sugar and gelatin. Stir thoroughly and let stand for a minute. Cook, stirring continuously, over water until slightly thickened. Remove from the heat and add the daiquiri mix (or limeade mix if daiquiri is unavailable). Chill in the refrigerator until partially set. Fold the whipped cream in gently and spread the filling over the baked crust. Sprinkle with grated lime rind and chill until firm.

Serves 6–8.

Here is a meal that will please the middle ground—those relatives who fall midway between Aunt Minnie and Auntie Mame. In this menu a good sturdy pork roast is much better for having had a furtive meeting with a bottle of Chianti. And the modest potatoes will offset anyone's suspicions concerning that glamorous spinach dish.

BOBO'S PORK ROAST CHIANTI
OVEN-ROASTED POTATOES
SPINACH PUDDING
MOCHA POLKA PIE

CHIANTI

BOBO'S PORK ROAST CHIANTI

4–5 pound pork roast
Salt and pepper
2 garlic cloves

2½ cups Chianti
2 tablespoons chopped parsley
3 potatoes

Rub the pork roast with salt and pepper. Make slits in it and fill with slivers of garlic. Place in a Dutch oven and roast uncovered in a 400-degree oven for 30 minutes. Add the wine and parsley to the pan and toss in 3 peeled, quartered potatoes. Cover pan and reduce heat to 350. Roast for 2½ hours more, basting frequently. Remove cover for the last 15 minutes. *Serves 6.*

SPINACH PUDDING

2 10-ounce packages frozen chopped spinach
2 cups cottage cheese, drained

1 teaspoon salt
⅓ cup grated Parmesan cheese
2 eggs

Cook spinach according to package directions and drain. Combine spinach, cottage cheese, salt, Parmesan cheese and eggs. Blend well and pour into a 1-quart casserole which has been well greased. Bake at 350 degrees for 30 minutes. *Serves 6.*

MOCHA POLKA PIE

1⅓ cups chocolate cookie crumbs
2 tablespoons sugar
¼ teaspoon cinnamon
⅓ cup melted butter
½ cup finely chopped almonds
1 cup sugar

½ cup water
3 egg whites, beaten until stiff
1 tablespoon instant coffee
⅛ teaspoon salt
2 cups heavy cream, whipped
½ cup slivered almonds
Shaved chocolate curls

Combine the cookie crumbs, sugar, cinnamon, melted butter and almonds. Stir until all crumbs are mixed in well. Press mixture against bottom and sides of a 9-inch pie pan. Chill thoroughly. Combine the 1 cup sugar and water in a saucepan; bring to a boil and cook rapidly until the syrup spins a thread (about 7 minutes or 242 degrees F. on a candy thermometer. Pour the syrup in a fine stream over the beaten egg whites, beating constantly. Continue beating until the meringue is thick and cool. Beat in the coffee and salt; fold in whipped cream and slivered almonds. Turn into pie shell and garnish with chocolate curls. Freeze several hours until firm. *Makes 1 9-inch pie to serve 6.*

All of this cooking may start you pointedly humming "Over the meadow and through the woods to Grandmother's house we go . . ." along about July next year, but do remember that even if virtue isn't its own reward it can lead you to a pretty good relationship with your family. And, having done your share, you won't hesitate for a moment to borrow your mother-in-law's garnets the next time you haul out your red velvet dress.

INDEX